Being a director

A practical guide to what you need to know

Being a director

A practical guide to what you need to know

Fourth Edition

By Margaret Morris-Marsham
of PricewaterhouseCoopers, Chartered Accountants

London, November 1998

Published by:

Gee Publishing Limited
100 Avenue Road
Swiss Cottage
London
NW3 3PG
Tel: +44 (171) 393 7400
Fax:+44 (171) 393 7463
Website: www.gee.co.uk

This book aims to provide general guidance only, and does not purport to deal with all possible questions and issues which may arise in any given situation. Should the reader encounter particular problems he/she is advised to seek professional advice, which PricewaterhouseCoopers would be pleased to provide.

No responsibility for loss occasioned to any person acting or refraining from action as a result of any material in this publication can be accepted by the author, copyright owner or publisher.

References throughout the book to *he/him/himself* should be understood to refer also to *she/her/herself.*

PricewaterhouseCoopers is authorised by the Institute of Chartered Accountants in England and Wales to carry on investment business.

ISBN 1 86089 039 3

First published 1988
Second edition 1991 both editions under the title Becoming a director?
Third edition 1993
Fourth Edition 1998

© PricewaterhouseCoopers, UK
  1998

Printed and bound in Great Britain by Alresford Press Ltd. Prospect Road, Alresford, Hants SO24 9QF

Acknowledgments

The guide was originally written by Stephen Copp and Alun Thomas and published in 1988 under the title of 'Becoming a director?' and has been extensively revised by Margaret Morris-Marsham, all of PricewaterhouseCoopers and predecessor firms. The assistance of Barry Johnson, Tony Bingham, Peter Holgate and other members of the firm in the preparation and revision of this book is gratefully appreciated. The assistance of ArnheimTite&Lewis, the correspondent law firm of PricewaterhouseCoopers, in connection with the revisions to Appendix II is also gratefully appreciated.

Contents

Chapter   **Page**

1   Introduction 1

2   Your company, its officers and management 9

3   Becoming a director 37

4   Your functions as a director 57

5   Your duties as a director to your company 65

6   Your duties to your co-directors 79

7   Your accounting and financial responsibilities 91

8   Shareholders' meetings 111

9   Your remuneration as a director 125

10 Loans to directors and other transactions 137

11 Your shareholding 155

12 Ceasing to be a director 163

13 Disqualification 173

14 Company investigations 187

15 Financial difficulties and company insolvency 195

Appendices

I   Why set up a company? 215

II   Your responsibilities to your employees 223

III   Table of requirements for a company's statutory books 241

IV   Section 214 of the Insolvency Act 1986 243

V   Table of criminal offences of which directors and other
      officers may be convicted 245

VI   Directors' loan decision tables 253

VII The Combined Code 257

Book list 279

Chapter 1

Introduction

Unlike other books on directors' responsibilities, this book is designed to answer the questions actually asked by company directors and some more that perhaps ought to be asked. Its question and answer format aims to make it easy to use. The book concentrates on questions that are mainly concerned with directors' responsibilities under company law.

The book should help a newly-appointed director to grasp a basic knowledge of his responsibilities and will be a useful refresher to many existing directors of their responsibilities. Company law contains many provisions that affect anyone who is a director of a limited company. We have not, however, attempted to cover all of the vast number of rules that apply to directors. In particular, in the pages available, we have not been able to cover tax and social security as they affect the director personally or as they affect his duty as a director.

This fourth edition has been updated for recent legislation. In particular, the new statutory rules for disclosure of directors' remuneration that came into effect for financial years ending on or after 31 March 1997 are discussed. The objective of these new rules was to provide, for listed companies, a measure of statutory underpinning for the disclosure requirements of the Listing Rules, to avoid duplication, and to change the disclosures for unlisted companies to a scaled-down version of the rules for the listed sector. The new rules also give effect to the recommendations of the Greenbury Committee to remove the requirement to show directors' emoluments in £5,000 bands and to review disclosure requirements for pensions information.

One of the most significant issues for directors responsibilities in recent years has been corporate governance. Three committees have been set up over the past six years leading to the publication of their reports. The Report of the Committee on the Financial Aspects of Corporate Governance ('the Cadbury Report') was published in December 1992 and Directors' Remuneration –

1

Report of a Study Group chaired by Sir Richard Greenbury ('the Greenbury Report') was published in July 1995. Finally, the Committee on Corporate Governance chaired by Sir Ronald Hampel published its final report ('the Hampel Report') in January 1998. These reports are aimed primarily at listed companies and many of their recommendations, through their inclusion in the listing rules, have become mandatory for listed companies. In June 1998 the recommendations of these reports were brought together when the Hampel Committee published 'The Combined Code – Principles of Good Governance and Code of Best Practice'. The Combined Code evolved from a review of the Cadbury and Greenbury provisions set out in the Hampel Committee report, but also included a number of small changes made by the London Stock Exchange following consultation.

In the period leading to the setting up of the Cadbury Committee in June 1991, there had been increasing concerns about the working of the corporate system, because of some unexpected failures of major companies and criticisms of the lack of effective board accountability for such matters as directors' pay.

The Cadbury Committee considered that to be effective boards must be free to drive their companies forward, but to exercise that freedom within a framework of effective accountability – this being the essence of any system of good corporate governance. The committee's recommendations concern the control and reporting functions of boards and the role of the auditors, but it sought by its proposals to contribute positively to promoting good corporate governance as a whole. The Committee defined 'corporate governance' as follows:

"Corporate governance is the system by which companies are directed and controlled. Boards of directors are responsible for the governance of their companies. The shareholders' role in governance is to appoint the directors and the auditors and to satisfy themselves that an appropriate governance structure is in place. The responsibilities of the board include setting the company's strategic aims, supervising the management of the business and reporting to shareholders on their stewardship. The board's actions are subject to laws, regulations and the shareholders in general meeting."

At the heart of the Committee's recommendations was a Code of Best Practice designed to achieve the necessary high standards of corporate behaviour in financial matters. The principles on which the Code was based were those of openness, integrity and accountability. The Committee recommended that listed companies should make a statement in their financial statements about their compliance with the Code giving reasons for any areas of non-compliance. They also recommended that the statement of compliance should be reviewed by the auditors before publication. The Committee also recommended that as many non-listed companies as possible should aim at meeting the Code's requirements.

The Greenbury Committee was set up in January 1995 to identity good practice in determining directors' remuneration in the light of some large pay increases, which gave rise to a wider concern about accountability for directors' remuneration. It saw the key to strengthening accountability as being the proper allocation of responsibility for determining directors' remuneration, proper reporting to shareholders and transparency. The purpose of the Greenbury Code of Best Practice was to set out best practice in determining and accounting for directors' remuneration and to replace the considerable number of codes and guidance notes that existed on the subject. The Committee recommended significant additional disclosure relating to directors' remuneration in companies' annual reports and for these to be introduced as continuing obligations by the Stock Exchange. The Listing Rules were amended to require listed companies, in their financial statements, to give detailed disclosure of all elements in the remuneration package of each individual director and to state whether they have complied with the best practice provisions of the Greenbury Code as to directors' remuneration.

Following the recommendations of the Cadbury and Greenbury committees, the Hampel Committee was established in November 1995 to review the implementation of their findings. The terms of its remit included to review the Cadbury Code, pursue any matters arising from the Greenbury Report, and keep under review the role and legal responsibilities of directors. The Hampel Committee considered that the importance of corporate governance lies in its contribution to business prosperity and to accountability. It also considered that accountability had preoccupied much public debate over the preceding years, and wished, therefore, to see the balance corrected in favour of the enhancement of prosperity. It was of the view that corporate governance needs broad principles and that all concerned should then apply these flexibly and with common sense to the varying circumstances of individual companies. It distinguished between principles of corporate governance and more detailed guidelines like the Cadbury and Greenbury Codes. The Committee considered that with a set of guidelines the question asked would be 'How are they complied with?'; whereas with principles, the question would be 'How are they applied in practice?'. What the Committee did not approve of was a box-ticking approach which it considered'neither fair nor likely to be efficient in preventing abuse'.

As promised by its Final Report, the Hampel Committee produced the Combined Code in June 1998. The Code contains both principles of good governance and a code of best practice with more detailed provisions. It embraces the Cadbury and, Greenbury Codes and Hampel's own work, and largely retains the substance of the two earlier codes. Section 1 of the Combined Code contains the corporate governance Principles and Code Provisions applicable to all listed companies incorporated in the United Kingdom. Section 2 contains Principles and Code Provisions applicable to institutional shareholders.

The Combined Code was passed to the Stock Exchange, which has published a new listing rule that applies to accounting periods ending on or after 31 December 1998. This rule requires listed companies to make a two-part disclosure statement in their annual reports about their compliance with the Combined Code. In the first part of their disclosure statement the company must include a narrative statement of how it has applied the 14 principles of good governance set out in section 1 of Part 1 of the Combined Code. It must also provide an explanation which enables its shareholders to evaluate how these principles have been applied. In the second part of the disclosure statement the company must state whether or not it has complied throughout the accounting period with the 45 code provisions set out in section 1 of part 2 of the Combined Code. Where the company has not complied with the code provisions, has only complied with some of the code provisions or has complied only for part of an accounting period, further disclosures must be made. The company must in these circumstances specify those code provisions with which it has not complied, state the period of the non-compliance and give reasons for the non-compliance. The company's statement in so far as it relates to certain Code provisions must be reviewed by the company's auditors.

The importance of corporate governance issues for directors will continue. In March 1998 the Department of Trade and Industry issued a consultation paper announcing a wide-ranging review of company law. One issue it identified was the relationship between company law and corporate governance. The government considers that, in general, the issues dealt with under the Combined Code are more suitable for best practice than legislation, provided that best practice is seen to be working, It suggested, however, that there may be a need for legislation in certain areas that are not covered by the new Code or where experience has shown that some legal underpinning is needed.

In addition, the Law Commission and Scottish Law Commission are currently reviewing the law regulating company directors' conflicts of interest and considering the case for a statutory statement of directors' duties under the general law. Further changes to the law relating to directors' responsibilities may, therefore, result in due course from the Government's review.

Your duties and responsibilities as a director, even of a small company, should now also be seen against the background of these reports. Many of their principles and recommendations are relevant to the aspects of being a director covered by this book and are discussed in the text. The Combined Code is set out in appendix VII.

We hope that you will find this book a useful and straightforward guide to the responsibilities you have undertaken as a director. This guidance is based on the law as at 15th October 1998.

Chapter 2

Your company, its officers and management

Question   *Page*

2.1   What is a company? 9

2.2   What role do directors play in the company? 9

2.3   What is a company's Memorandum of association? 10

2.4   What are a company's Articles of association? 12

2.5   Should the Articles of association make special provision for directors, or will Table A do? 13

2.6   What are a company's statutory books? 14

2.7   What is a company's registered office? 15

2.8   What name can a company have? 16

2.9   Does a company have to trade under its registered name? 17

2.10 Can a company change its registered name? 17

2.11 What is a company's common seal? 18

2.12 What legal provisions apply to companies? 18

2.13 Who owns a company? 21

2.14 Who runs a company? 21

2.15 Who are a company's officers? 22

2.16 What is the significance of being a company officer? 22

2.17 Does a company need to have a company secretary? 23

2.18 Who can be a company secretary? 23

2.19 Does a company secretary also have to be a director? 24

2.20 What are the company secretary's responsibilities? 24

2.21 What happens when the company secretary is absent? 25

2.22 Does a company have to appoint an auditor? 25

2.23 What companies do not need to appoint auditors? 26

2.24 How does a company appoint an auditor? 27

2.25 Who can be a company's auditor? 27

2.26 Can a company change its auditor? 28

2.27 What is an audit? 29

2.28 What does the auditor do? 30

2.29 What other benefits can an audit provide? 31

2.30 Does a company have to have a solicitor? 32

2.31 Who is the Registrar of Companies and what does it mean to
      'file' documents with him? 32

2.32 What documents must be filed with the Registrar of
      Companies? 33

Your company, its officers and management

2.1 What is a company?

A company is a person from a legal point of view, albeit an artificial one. The Companies Act 1985 states:

> *"From the date of incorporation mentioned in the certificate* [of incorporation], *the subscribers of the memorandum* [of association], *together with such other persons as may from time to time become members of the company, shall be a body corporate by the name contained in the memorandum* [of association]. *"*

So, the company is recognised by the law as being a separate legal person from both its directors and shareholders. Although the law has developed an increasing number of exceptions to this rule, it still generally holds fast.

In most cases a director will be appointed to a company which is already formed and trading. A company will be a company limited by shares if the liability of its shareholders is limited by the memorandum to the amount, if any, unpaid on their shares. Companies limited by shares are by far the most common type and, unless otherwise stated, this book refers to such companies throughout.

2.2 What role do directors play in the company?

Sometimes, however, it will be necessary to form a company, for instance, where the director will be the major shareholder as well. For such directors, Appendix I gives a brief explanation of the advantages and disadvantages of incorporation and of how a company is formed. When you become a director of a company, whether large or small, whether family or not, you take on the task of preserving and enhancing the shareholders' investment in it and, with this task, major duties and responsibilities. It is with these duties and responsibilities that this book is concerned.

The introduction of the Insolvency Act 1986 was the beginning of the enforcement by the courts of higher standards for directors. Together with the Company Directors Disqualification Act 1986, it forms a powerful tool in the hands of liquidators to take action against directors whose conduct they consider falls below the required standard. In many of the cases that have been decided over the last few years the directors involved have generally (without being dishonest) shown incompetence or a disregard for the basic requirements of company law, for example, by failing to keep records or prepare annual accounts or by misapplying company assets, and have, as a consequence, been ordered by the courts to contribute to the assets of the insolvent company.

In addition, there was continuing concern about standards of financial reporting by listed companies and the accountability of their directors. This led to the setting up of the Cadbury Committee in May 1991, the Greenbury Group in January 1995 and the Hampel Committee in November 1995. Their aim was to raise standards by setting out principles and codes of best practice which boards could follow. The two part disclosure statement recommended in the Hampel Combined Code and now a requirement following a change to the Listing Rules, further raises the standards expected of listed companies (see chapter 1).

There is, therefore, a significant amount of practical guidance on how directors should carry out their roles. You, as a director, are not expected to act as an expert (unless you are one), but you should know sufficient about the legal duties and responsibilities concerned with the office of director to enable you to discharge these duties and responsibilities properly and to know when to take professional advice.

2.3 What is a company's Memorandum of association?

The Memorandum of association (usually bound with the Articles of association when printed) is a document which primarily sets out the purpose of a company. It must state:

■   The company's name.

■   Whether the registered office of the company is to be situated in England and Wales, or in Scotland.

■   The company's objects.

■   That the liability of the company's members is limited.

■   The amount of share capital that the company proposes to be registered with and its division into shares.

The most important clause is the one that sets out the company's objects. Companies are usually formed for some specific purpose or purposes. Company law intends these purposes to be crystallised in the objects clause. One of the more common reasons why a company is specially formed and not purchased off-the-shelf is because the objects clause needs to be individually drafted. The importance of the objects clause derives from the legal rule of *ultra vires*. This rule means that where a company acts outside its capacity, that is, outside the objects or powers given to it in its Memorandum of association, that act is void. For various legal reasons this rule is of less importance nowadays to persons dealing with a company, partly because objects clauses are so widely drafted that they give a company power to do almost anything that a natural person could do. Also, such wide objects clauses are included as a matter of course in the Memorandum of association of companies purchased off-the-shelf.

However, the Companies Act 1989 makes it possible to have a general commercial company whose object is to carry on any trade or business whatsoever, and with the power to do all such things as are incidental or conducive to the carrying on of any trade or business. The Act also amends the provisions concerning the *ultra vires* rule in the Companies Act 1985 and these amended provisions will further limit the ability of a company to back out of a transaction on the ground that it is outside the company's capacity. This will give greater protection to third parties. Although the *ultra vires* rule will be effectively abolished for external purposes (that is, in connection with the company's dealings with third parties), the provisions in the 1989 Act will not affect any liability directors may incur as a result of any breach of duty arising from their acting outside the company's capacity.

Directors should still ensure that the company only enters into transactions that are permitted by its memorandum and that they themselves act within the authority given to them under the Articles of association. Otherwise, they may incur personal liability. The duty of a director to act within his powers is dealt with more fully in paragraph 5.2.

2.4 What are a company's Articles of association?

A company's Articles of association are, in effect, its rule book, dealing with the detailed rules of the company's internal administration. Generally, the management of a company's affairs is delegated by the Articles of association to the directors. They may, therefore, have quite extensive powers to conduct the company's business without the need to seek shareholders' approval. On incorporation, a company may be registered with its own Articles of association or, more commonly, it need not register any. In that situation 'Table A', which is a specimen set of Articles of association, will be adopted as the company's own. Table A can be found in Statutory Instrument (SI) 1985 No 805, Companies (Tables A to F) Regulations 1985. Frequently, companies will base their Articles of association on Table A, but include their own modifications to it.

The current Table A deals with the following matters:

- The company's share capital.
- Company meetings.
- The number of directors.
- Alternate directors.
- The powers of directors.
- The delegation of directors' powers.
- The appointment and retirement of directors.
- The disqualification and removal of directors.
- The remuneration of directors.
- Directors' expenses.
- Directors' appointments and interests.
- Directors' gratuities and pensions.

- Directors' meetings.
- The company secretary.
- Minutes of meetings.
- The company's seal.
- Dividends and the capitalisation of profits.
- Accounts.

You will appreciate from this that it is a good idea for you to familiarise yourself with the particular Articles of association of a company before accepting appointment as a director of it.

2.5 Should the Articles of association make special provision for directors, or will Table A do?

Obviously, the answer to this question will depend on the particular circumstances of your company. Areas which commonly require consideration are:

- Whether, in the case of a private company, the company is to be permitted to have a sole director.

- Whether any maximum number of directors is to be specified.

- Whether the directors' right to exercise the company's power of borrowing should be limited in any way.

- Whether any special voting rights are to be conferred on any director(s).

- Whether a special *quorum* is desirable for board meetings (see question 6.2).

- Whether directors should have to retire by rotation and, if so, how (see question 12.6).

- Whether directors have the power to appoint an alternate director (see question 3.7).

- Whether the directors can appoint associate directors (see question 3.6), who are not directors for legal purposes.

- In the case of private companies, whether to give the directors power to refuse to register a transfer of shares.

- Whether the directors are to have the power to dismiss a director independently of the company in general meeting.

As a result of the recommendations on corporate governance in the Cadbury, Greenbury and Hampel Reports brought together in the Combined Code issued in June 1998, the following areas could also be considered:

- Constitution of audit committees (see question 6.13 and 7.17), remuneration and nomination committees (see question 6.13).

- Powers to appoint and remove company secretary (see question 2.20).

- Schedule of matters reserved to the main board of directors for decision (see question 4.1).

- Rights of directors to take independent professional advice in the furtherance of their duties at the company's expense.

2.6 What are a company's statutory books?

When you purchase a company off-the-shelf you will usually receive a number of impressive-looking bound books, referred to as the company's 'statutory books', which have to be kept by law. There are different rights of inspection, restrictions on the location of registers and permissible charges for inspection for each 'statutory book'. These are summarised in appendix III.

The different 'statutory books' which must be kept are:

- The register of interests in shares
  Public companies must maintain a register of their 'substantial shareholders', that is, holders of three per cent or more of the nominal value of the shares having voting rights who have notified their

holdings in accordance with the Companies Act 1985. (There are certain exceptions where the obligation to notify only arises when the holdings are equal to or more than ten per cent, for instance holdings of investment managers.)

■ The register of directors and secretaries
The obligation to maintain this is considered in question 3.14.

■ The register of directors' interests in shares and debentures
The obligation to maintain this is considered in question 11.8.

■ The register of members
All companies must keep a register giving details of their shareholders.

■ The minute book
Minutes must be kept of shareholders', directors' and managers' meetings (see question 6.14).

■ The register of charges
All companies must keep a register giving details of all charges on company property and assets.

■ The register of debenture holders
In fact, this is the only statutory book that a company is not obliged by law to keep. However, if a company does keep such a register it must be available for inspection.

In addition, directors' service contracts must be kept available for inspection (see question 3.18).

2.7 What is a company's registered office?

When a company is formed you need to give the location of the company's 'registered office' on Form 10 to be filed with the Registrar of companies (Registrar). Furthermore, the company's Memorandum of Association must state whether the registered office of the company is to be situated in England and Wales, or Scotland.

The registered office of a company does not need to be the company's principal place of business, but may, for example, be its accountant's or solicitor's address, provided that the accountant or solicitor has agreed that the premises may be used as the registered office.

The main function of a company's registered office is to provide an official address for the company, in particular, for the service of legal documents. It is particularly important, therefore, where a company changes its location, that it notifies the Registrar on Form No. 287 or Form 287(I) of the change of its registered office. The change takes effect upon the notice being registered by the Registrar and the company has 14 days from the date it gives notice to the Registrar to act on the change. It should be remembered that the company has a duty to keep certain registers at its registered office (see appendix III) and to mention the address of its registered office on business letters and order forms.

2.8 What name can a company have?

A company can be registered with any name subject to certain minimal restrictions:

- A company will not be registered with a name which duplicates or is too similar to the name of an existing company. However, the fact that the registration of a particular name is accepted is not conclusive of the company's right to be registered under that name. The DTI can order a company to change its name within twelve months of it being registered, if it considers that its name is the same as or too similar to that of an existing company name. Furthermore, if the effect of registering such a name is to mislead the public into believing that the company's business is that of another company, the courts may regard this as 'passing off'. In such a situation, the court could grant an injunction to stop the use of the name as well as either an award of damages or an account of profits from using the name.

- A company will not be registered with a name which is offensive or which would constitute a criminal offence. Where a name is sensitive for some reason (for example, because it implies a connection with the government) the permission of the DTI is required. Furthermore, a company may be ordered to change its name if the DTI considers that it gives so misleading an indication of the company's business as to be likely to cause harm to the public

■ If the company is a private limited company its name *must* end with 'limited' or 'ltd.'. If it is a public company (see appendix I paragraph (iii)) its name *must* end with 'public limited company' or 'plc'. These words must appear only at the *end* of the company's name. Where the sole objects of a company limited by guarantee are to promote commerce, art, science, education, religion, charity or a profession and its constitution requires *inter alia* its income to be applied for those objects and not distributed to members, the word 'limited' may be omitted.

Companies House has issued a helpful booklet 'Choosing a company name' (CHN 2) in its Notes for Guidance series.

2.9   Does a company have to trade under its registered name?

No. Frequently, for example, a company which is acquired off-the-shelf may have an unusual name. Rather than change the company's name it is common for the company to trade under a business name. If it does so, the company will be subject to the Business Names Act 1985. This requires disclosure of the company's registered name on business correspondence and at any business premises. It also prohibits the use of certain names and requires approval of others.

2.10   Can a company change its registered name?

Yes. To do so the company's shareholders must pass a special resolution, subject to similar considerations as to the choice of name on first registration (see above). It is usual upon a change of name for the company's Memorandum of Association to be altered and a footnote added to explain the change of name. Following the passing of the special resolution for the change of name the company will need to obtain a new Certificate of Incorporation from the Registrar. The change of name takes effect from the date of the new certificate and the company should not use the new name until this date. The Registrar charges a fee for changes of name and, by paying a premium for this service, companies can request the Registrar to effect a name change on a same-day basis.

2.11 What is a company's common seal?

As mentioned in question 2.1, a company is an artificial person. The company's common seal can be regarded as that person's signature. When an off-the-shelf company is purchased, a seal, which is a metal stamp with the company's name engraved on it, will usually be acquired at the same time. It is usual for the seal to be adopted and impressed in the company's minute book at the first directors' meeting.

The common seal is only required to be impressed upon a document which has to be under seal if executed by a natural person, that is, a deed. When the seal is used in this way Table A requires that it is evidenced by the signatures of a director and either the company secretary or a second director. In practice, the common seal is impressed on a variety of documents (for example, commercial contracts) and the company secretary will record in a 'seal book' details of when it is used.

However, the Companies Act 1989 abolished the necessity for a company to have a common seal. It provides that a document signed by a director and the secretary of the company, or by two directors of a company, and expressed (in whatever form of words) to be executed by the company, has the same effect as if executed under the common seal of the company.

Many companies which have a common seal may still decide, as a matter of policy, to continue to use the seal when executing documents.

2.12 What legal provisions apply to companies?

If this book were a thousand pages long it still might not be possible to answer this question fully! The law applicable to companies derives from a number of sources – statute, the decisions of the courts and, increasingly, directly effective provisions of European Community law. On top of this, there is a mass of regulations that companies have to follow, for example, Financial Reporting Standards, Statements of Standard Accounting Practice, and, in the case of listed companies, the Listing Rules of the Stock Exchange.

The Listing Rules set out the rules that companies applying to be listed on the London Stock Exchange must follow in making their application and the various continuing obligations they must comply with afterwards. The main categories of legislation that you will need to consider are as follows:

Company law

The principal pieces of legislation you need to be aware of are:

- The Companies Act 1985

  This Act is the main codification of company law. It deals with:
  - The formation of companies.
  - Company names.
  - Company powers.
  - The increase, maintenance and reduction of a company's share capital.
  - Accounting and auditing requirements.
  - Company management – the qualifications, duties and responsibilities of directors and secretaries.
  - The enforcement of fair dealing by directors.
  - Company investigations.
  - The protection of a company's members against unfair prejudice.

- The Companies Act 1989
  This *inter alia* amends certain provisions of the Companies Act 1985, particularly in relation to accounts and audit, the *ultra vires* rule and investigations. It also abolished the need for a company to have a common seal and introduced the written resolution procedure and the elective regime for private companies.

- The Company Directors Disqualification Act 1986
  This Act is dealt with in chapter 13. Its purpose is self-explanatory.

- The Insolvency Act 1986
  This Act deals with:
  - Company voluntary arrangements.
  - Administration orders.

- ■ Receivership.
- ■ Winding up of companies.

■ **The Criminal Justice Act 1993 – Part V**
The Company Securities (Insider Dealing) Act 1985 has now been replaced by Part V of the above Act. The implications for directors of the insider dealing provisions are summarised in question 11.9.

■ **The Financial Services Act 1986**
Under this Act various organisations were set up to regulate and control companies and other entities that undertake investment business. The Act will be amended to take account of the Government's proposals to put in place a new regulatory system for the financial services industry. Many of the regulatory powers under the Act were delegated to the Securities and Investments Board (SIB). In October 1997 the Financial Services Authority (FSA) was launched and continues to exercise all the functions which the SIB had under the Act. The Financial Services and Markets Bill, published in mid 1998, when enacted will create a new statutory regime. Under this the FSA will assume full responsibility for the work currently undertaken by the existing financial sector regulators and will become the 'super regulator' of financial services, banking, building societies, friendly societies and insurance companies.

■ **The Theft Act 1968**
Although the title of this Act may not make it seem immediately relevant, it deals with:
- ■ Certain offences of fraud, such as false accounting.
- ■ The liability of company officers for offences by the company.
- ■ False statements by company directors.

Tax law

All companies and their directors are well advised to seek professional advice on how tax law affects them.

Employment law

A brief overview of your responsibilities in law to your employees is given in appendix II.

Other

As you will appreciate there are hundreds of other obligations the law lays upon companies and their directors which cannot be described in detail in this book. Examples are the consumer protection legislation, the law of landlord and tenant and environmental law. The Institute of Directors has published a valuable book on this subject called Directors' Personal Liabilities in the Corporate Governance Series, which is a useful starting point. In addition, some specialised businesses are subject to additional regulation. For example, insurance companies are regulated by the Insurance Companies Act 1982. This book only considers the position of ordinary companies.

There are many publications the aim of which is to help directors through the maze of legislation that affects them. See the Book List at the end of this book.

2.13 Who owns a company?

A company is owned by its shareholders. However, you must not confuse this type of ownership with the ownership of the company's assets. Because a company is a separate legal entity, the company itself owns its assets. A shareholder does not even have an insurable interest in the assets of his company – the assets belong to the company and not to the shareholders.

2.14 Who runs a company?

Lord Denning summarised the responsibility for managing a company in this way:

> *"A company may in many ways be likened to a human body. It has a brain and nerve centre which controls what it does. It also has hands which hold the tools and act in accordance with directions from the centre. Some of the people in the company*

are mere servants and agents who are nothing more than hands to do the work and cannot be said to represent the mind or will. Others are directors and managers who represent the directing mind and will of the company and control what it does. The state of mind of these managers is the state of mind of the company and is treated by the law as such. So you will find in cases where the law requires personal fault as a condition of liability in tort, the fault of the manager will be the personal fault of the company, ... So also in the criminal law, in cases where the law requires a guilty mind as a condition of a criminal offence, the guilty mind of the directors or the managers will render the company itself guilty ..... Whether their intention is the company's intention depends on the nature of the matter under consideration, the relative position of the officer or agent, and the other relevant facts and circumstances of the case."

The important question then is 'Who are a company's officers?'

2.15 Who are a company's officers?

The Companies Act 1985 defines the officers of a company as including the directors, managers and the company secretary. The courts have also taken the view that the company's auditor should usually be regarded as an officer. A company's bankers and solicitors will not usually be officers, unless they have other duties and, consequently, occupy a position in the company different from that of a normal banker or solicitor.

2.16 What is the significance of being a company officer?

The officers of a company are those who are regarded by the law as being accountable for it. For example, many of the criminal offences contained in the Companies Act 1985 may be committed by any officer of the company, although some apply only to directors (see appendix V). Furthermore, the financial statements of a company must disclose various transactions with a company's officers. (see question 10.12).

2.17 Does a company need to have a company secretary?

Yes. This is a legal requirement for every company. However, you can obtain company secretarial services from most firms of chartered accountants or solicitors.

2.18 Who can be a company secretary?

Anyone can be the company secretary of a private company. In a typical small company it will be usual for there to be two directors, one of whom is also appointed company secretary (see also question 2.19).

In the case of a public company, the directors must take all reasonable steps to secure that the secretary of the company has the requisite knowledge and experience to discharge the functions of company secretary. Furthermore, to be eligible to be company secretary of a public company, a person must satisfy one of the following conditions. He must:

- Have been company secretary, or assistant or deputy company secretary on 22 December 1980 to the company in question.

- Have been the company secretary of a public company for at least three of the five years immediately preceding his appointment.

- Be a member of any of the following:

    - The Institute of Chartered Accountants in England and Wales.
    - The Institute of Chartered Accountants of Scotland.
    - The Chartered Association of Certified Accountants.
    - The Institute of Chartered Accountants in Ireland.
    - The Institute of Chartered Secretaries and Administrators.
    - The Chartered Institute of Cost and Management Accountants.
    - The Chartered Institute of Public Finance and Accountancy.

- Be a barrister, advocate or solicitor called or admitted in any part of the UK.

- Be a person who, either because he holds or has held any other position or because he is a member of any other body, appears to the directors to be capable of discharging the functions of a company secretary.

2.19 Does a company secretary also have to be a director?

No. Although it is usual in small private companies it is not a legal requirement. A private company must have at least one director, but the same person cannot be the sole director and company secretary.

2.20 What are the company secretary's responsibilities?

As noted in question 2.15, a company secretary is an officer of the company. He may also be a director and/or an employee of the company. The role of the company secretary has become increasingly important as the legal regulation of companies has developed. For example, some company secretaries provide guidance to the board of directors on their statutory responsibilities. Traditionally, the company secretary has been responsible for company administration. His duties include the convening of board and company meetings on the direction of the board, taking minutes of meetings, writing up the company's statutory books, and filing returns with the Registrar. Unless the company uses external share registrars, the company secretary will also deal with share transfers. Because of the legal nature of the role, frequently a company secretary will be a solicitor or barrister, who will be involved in other aspects of the company's legal work (for example, negotiating and drafting contracts, ensuring patents and copyrights are protected and dealing with employment law questions). As Lord Denning put it, the company secretary:

> "..... is an officer of the company with extensive duties and responsibilities ..... He is no longer a mere clerk. He regularly makes representations on behalf of the company and enters into contracts on its behalf which come within the day to day running of the company's business, so much so that he may be regarded as held out as having authority to do such things on behalf of the company. He is certainly entitled to sign contracts connected with the administrative side of a company's affairs, such as employing staff, and ordering cars, and so forth. All

such matters now come within the ostensible authority of a company secretary."

The importance of the company secretary's position is endorsed by the Combined Code which says that he has a key role to play in ensuring board procedures are both followed and regularly reviewed and that any question of his removal should be a matter for the board as a whole (see Combined Code A.1.4).

2.21 What happens when the company secretary is absent? Can a company appoint an assistant company secretary to take over?

Only the company secretary can validly perform the duties of the company secretary. The Companies Act 1985 permits an assistant or deputy company secretary to do so, but only where there is no company secretary or none capable of acting. To avoid the difficulties that this may cause, the Companies Act 1985 permits a company to appoint more than one person as company secretary, who then act as joint secretaries. However, this would generally be necessary and practicable only where the duties of the company secretary are particularly onerous.

2.22 Does a company have to appoint an auditor?

Yes, a company must appoint auditors for each financial year. Where the company is newly incorporated an auditor must be appointed, either by the directors, or if they fail to do so, by the shareholders at any time before the first general meeting of the company at which the accounts are laid. It is, however, general practice to do so at the first board meeting to ensure the matter is not overlooked. This auditor holds office only until the end of the first general meeting at which the company's financial statements are presented, and he may then be reappointed. However, some very small companies and dormant companies are exempt from having their financial statements audited and will not need to appoint an auditor (see question 2.23).

An existing company must appoint an auditor at each general meeting it holds where its annual financial statements are presented. This normally happens at the company's annual general meeting. The auditor will then hold office until the next such meeting. If, for any reason, the company ceases to have an auditor between meetings, the directors, (or if they fail to do so, the shareholders) may appoint a new auditor.

If a private company has elected, by passing an elective resolution, (see question 8.14) to dispense with the laying of financial statements before the company in general meeting, auditors must be appointed in general meeting before the end of the period of 28 days from the date on which copies of the annual financial statements for the previous financial year are sent to members (Companies Act 1985 Section 385A). A private company may also elect, by elective resolution, to dispense with the annual appointment of auditors by following the statutory procedure in accordance with section 386. Whilst such an elective resolution is in force, the auditors will be deemed to be reappointed for each succeeding financial year on expiry of the time for appointing auditors under section 385A, until the resolution is revoked by the company passing an ordinary resolution revoking it.

If for any reason a company has no auditor, the Secretary of State for Trade and Industry must be notified within a week, and he may then appoint an auditor himself.

2.23 What companies do not need to appoint auditors?

Certain small companies do not have to appoint auditors. There are two instances where such a company is exempt from the obligation to appoint auditors. First, a small company need not appoint auditors if it qualifies as dormant, that is, it has not, during the year, had any transactions that need to be entered into its accounting records (see question 7.6 for what accounting records a company must keep). A dormant company may pass a resolution under section 250 of the Companies Act 1985 not to appoint auditors; it will then be exempt from this requirement and the requirement to have its accounts audited. It will cease to be exempt if it stops being dormant.

Secondly, a small company with a turnover in the year of not more than £350,000 and a balance sheet total (basically total assets) of not more than £1.4m is exempt under section 249A from appointing auditors and having its accounts for that year audited. However public companies, banks, insurance companies, registered insurance brokers and financial services companies cannot take the exemption. In addition, the rules are more complicated where the small company is a subsidiary or parent company and different rules apply where the company is a charity. When they take this exemption, the directors must make a statement on the balance sheet acknowledging their responsibilities for the financial statements (see question 7.2).

2.24 How does a company appoint an auditor?

The first auditors of a newly incorporated company may be appointed by the board of directors. An ordinary resolution of the company's shareholders is all that is needed to reappoint an existing auditor or an auditor appointed by the directors as its first auditor, although special notice is required to reappoint a company's first auditor. The auditor should send you an 'engagement letter' which is intended to define clearly the extent of the auditor's responsibilities and, therefore, to minimise the risk of any misunderstanding in the work that he may carry out. It is useful for a company's directors to discuss the contents of the engagement letter with the proposed auditor *prior* to his appointment, because the letter of engagement will form the basis of the contract between the company and the auditor. Accordingly, you should confirm your agreement to the engagement letter in writing. Subsequent regular review of the engagement letter helps the directors and the auditor avoid misunderstandings regarding the company's audit.

2.25 Who can be a company's auditor?

Usually, only an individual or firm authorised to carry out company audits by one of the following bodies may be appointed:

- The Institute of Chartered Accountants in England and Wales.
- The Institute of Chartered Accountants of Scotland.
- The Institute of Chartered Accountants in Ireland.
- The Chartered Association of Certified Accountants.
- The Association of Authorised Public Accountants.

Under special circumstances, usually involving DTI approval, a person who is not a member of one of these bodies may be an auditor, but this is very rare.

More importantly, certain persons who are connected in some way with a company are prohibited by law from being the company's auditor. These include:

- A director of the company.
- The company secretary.
- An employee of the company.

In all these situations a partner or employee of the person is also prohibited from being the company's auditor or from acting as auditor of any group company. Any person who acts as an auditor knowing that he is disqualified from appointment commits a criminal offence.

From 1991 only 'registered auditors' have been able to audit companies incorporated in the UK. A registered auditor is a sole practice, a partnership or a corporate practice which has been registered by a Recognised Supervisory Body, for example the Institute of Chartered Accountants in England and Wales, as eligible to accept audit appointments.

2.26 Can a company change its auditor?

Yes, but for obvious reasons, the law makes this difficult to do without his agreement.

Special notice (see question 8.7) is required for a resolution to be put to a general meeting of a company to remove an auditor before the end of his period of office or to appoint an auditor other than the retiring auditor. This also applies if the resolution put to a general meeting is to fill a casual vacancy in the office of auditor or to reappoint a retiring auditor who was appointed by the directors to fill a casual vacancy.

A copy of this resolution has to be sent to the proposed auditor and also to the retiring or resigning auditor who is not proposed for reappointment. The retiring auditor not proposed for reappointment is entitled to make written representations to the company and require the company to circulate these to shareholders. If this is not done, the auditor may require them to be read out at general meeting.

When an auditor ceases to hold office for any reason he must deposit at the company's registered office a statement of any circumstances connected to his ceasing to hold office which he considers should be brought to the attention of members or creditors of the company. The company must then send a copy of the statement to members within 14 days unless, on application to the court, the court holds the statement to be defamatory. Even if the auditor considers there are no circumstances which should be brought to the members' attention he must deposit a statement that there are none. In any event the company must send a copy of the auditors' notice of resignation to the Registrar within 14 days.

You will also find that the new auditor is required, as a matter of professional etiquette, to write to the outgoing auditor seeking information that could influence his decision as to whether or not he may properly accept appointment. This provides a sanction against companies who might wish to change their auditor for other than good reasons.

If a company does adopt a resolution to remove an auditor before his term of office expires, the company must give notice on the prescribed form to the Registrar within 14 days.

2.27 What is an audit?

The explanatory foreword to Auditing Standards and Auditing Guidelines says that:

> *"An 'audit' is the independent examination of, and expression of an opinion on, the financial statements of an enterprise... The auditor's responsibility is to report on the financial statements as presented by management."*

The auditor's report will include an unqualified opinion when in the auditors' judgment the financial statements give a true and fair view and have been prepared in accordance with relevant accounting or other requirements. Where these criteria are not met, the auditor may issue a qualified opinion, an adverse opinion or a disclaimer of opinion, depending on the circumstances, if, after discussions, he has not been able to agree with you the amendments he believes are necessary.

An audit carried out in accordance with Auditing Standards is designed to provide reasonable assurance that the financial statements as a whole are free from material misstatement, whether caused by error or by fraud.

2.28 What does the auditor do?

Under the Companies Act 1985 a company's auditor has certain duties. The auditor has to make a report to the company's shareholders stating whether, in his opinion, the financial statements have been properly prepared in accordance with the Act and in particular whether they give a true and fair view. The auditor must also state in his report by exception if he considers that proper accounting records have not been kept or if the information given in the directors' report is not consistent with the financial statements. In addition, if the financial statements do not contain the information required by the Act regarding directors' remuneration, loans to directors or other transactions they have with the company, the auditor must disclose this information so far as he is able.

The 1985 Act clearly lays the responsibility for the preparation of the financial statements on the directors. A company's auditor is not responsible for their preparation; he only has to report on them. The term 'true and fair' is not defined by law. There will, in any one instance, generally be more than one true and fair view and the auditor is, therefore, giving an opinion on whether the financial statements, as prepared by the directors, give a true and fair view.

To assist auditors to carry out their statutory duties, there are Statements of Auditing Standards, Practice Notes and Bulletins, issued by the Auditing Practices Board (formerly the Auditing Practices Committee) and other auditing guidance issued by professional bodies. The purpose of these is to establish standards and provide guidance as to the procedures auditors should carry out in performing their work to a satisfactory quality. Auditors do not have responsibility to prevent or detect fraud. This remains with management. Statement of Auditing Standard 110 – Fraud and error – clarifies the auditor's position on this point and states that it is not the auditor's function to prevent fraud and error. However, auditors should design their work so as to have a reasonable expectation of detecting misstatements arising from fraud or error, which are material to the financial statements.

An auditor has a right to attend and be heard at general meetings and a right of access to the company's books, accounts and vouchers. In addition, he can require the company's officers to give them such information and explanations as they think necessary for the performance of his duties as auditor. It is an offence for an officer to make a statement (oral or written) to the auditor which is misleading, false or deceptive in a material particular.

After an auditor has been appointed he will set out the terms of his appointment in an engagement letter agreed with his client. He will plan how to perform the audit efficiently so as to obtain sufficient reliable evidence as to whether there is a material error in the financial statements. This will include obtaining information about the business, its areas of risk and the accounting policies the company follows. The auditor will obtain an understanding of the company's accounting systems to establish whether they provide a reliable basis for drawing up the financial statements. The auditor will, then, allocate staff to the audit and arrange visits to the client aimed at meeting the client's timetable.

Audit evidence will be sought by observing the company's financial systems, the way operations are carried out and by inspecting evidence such as invoices and statements as well as the company's books. The amount of evidence sought will depend on the risk of error. The auditor will seek independent confirmation and representations from third parties where he considers it appropriate.

Beside having the benefit of a second opinion on the company's financial statements, the directors can obtain other benefits from the audit. The auditor usually has considerable experience and expertise in financial matters. He can, therefore, quite outside the audit report he is required to give by law, comment usefully on certain aspects of the company's activities from the information obtained during the audit.

2.29 What other benefits can an audit provide?

In the course of his audit your auditor will have the opportunity to look into your company's business in depth. Because of his independence from his clients and because of his technical skills, an auditor is well-placed to advise on aspects of financial reporting that go beyond his required role of giving an opinion on financial statements. He is likely to be able, for instance, to advise on accounting treatments most suited to the business and on the best accounting practice or current trends in disclosure. The giving of advice on general trends or practice need in no way contravene the duty of confidentiality which an auditor owes to each of his clients. The subject of 'Added value to the external audit' was covered in more detail by the Auditing Practices Committee in an *Audit Brief* (1990) written by Roger Davis of PricewaterhouseCoopers

2.30 Does a company have to have a solicitor?

There is no legal requirement for a company to appoint a solicitor, as there is for it to appoint an auditor. In fact, there is no specific office as such that a solicitor could be appointed to, although clearly a solicitor can be appointed to general offices, such as director or company secretary. However, it is common for a company to deal with most of its legal business through one firm of solicitors, so that they have an opportunity to gain an understanding of the company's business and needs.

2.31 Who is the Registrar of Companies and what does it mean to 'file' documents with him?

At various places in this book you will come across references to 'filing' or 'delivering' documents with or to the 'Registrar'. The Registrar of Companies for England and Wales is responsible for companies whose registered office is in England or Wales. There is a separate Registrar of Companies for Scotland who is responsible for companies whose registered office is in Scotland.

■   The address of the Registrar of Companies for England and Wales is:
     Companies House
     Crown Way
     Cardiff CF4 3UZ
     Tel: 01222-380801

- The address of the Registrar of Companies for Scotland is:
  Companies House
  37 Castle Terrace
  Edinburgh EH1 2EB
  Tel: 0131-535 5800

- Additional facilities for personal inspection of company records are maintained at:
  Companies House,
  55-71 City Road,
  London EC1Y 1BB.
  Tel: 0171-253 9393
  and also at satellite offices in Leeds, Manchester, Birmingham and Glasgow. The Internet address of Companies House is http\\www.companieshouse.gov.uk. However, these inspection facilities are not available on the Internet. The London office of Companies House is expected to move to a new address in the autumn of 1998. All telephone enquiries are dealt with from Cardiff on 01222 380801.

To file a document, it is simply necessary to send it to the Registrar at the appropriate address.

2.32 What documents must be filed with the Registrar of Companies?

There are a vast number of documents that may have to be filed with the Registrar, depending upon your company's circumstances. The principal ones that you are likely to need to consider are:

- The company formation documents (see appendix I paragraph (ii)).

- The notice of change of directors or secretaries or in their particulars (Form 288(c)). This will need to be filed, for example, if a director changes his address.

- The annual return of a company (Form 363a, 363b or 363s).

- Particulars of a mortgage or charge (Form 395).

■ The forms relating to changing from private to public company status (Forms 43(3), 43(3)(e) and 117).

■ Notice of the alteration of a company's accounting reference date (Form 225). A company incorporated on or after 1st April 1996 is automatically given an accounting reference date which is the last day of the month in which the anniversary of its incorporation falls. Accounting reference dates are discussed in paragraph 7.18.

Chapter 3

Becoming a director

Question   *Page*

3.1   Am I eligible to be a director? 37

3.2   How many directors should a company have? 38

3.3   What should I find out about a company before accepting
appointment? 38

3.4   Can I hold more than one directorship? 42

3.5   I already do the same job as the other directors and attend
board meetings. Am I in fact a director? 43

3.6   I've been promoted to 'director of marketing'.
I am a real director, aren't I? 43

3.7   I've been asked to be an 'alternate director'.
What does that mean? 44

3.8   What are the formalities attached to being appointed
an alternate director? 45

3.9   I've been asked to be a 'nominee director'.
What does that mean? 45

3.10 I've heard of 'shadow directors'. What are they? 46

3.11 What are the implications of being a shadow director? 46

3.12 I've been asked to be a 'non-executive director' of a company.
       What does this entail? 47

3.13 I've heard some non-executive directors are called independent.
       Is this distinction important? 48

3.14 Are there any formalities on being appointed a director? 49

3.15 If I become a director of a company will I be one of its
       employees? 50

3.16 Should I have a service contract with my company? 50

3.17 What terms should be included in my service contract? 50

3.18 Will the shareholders be able to see any of the terms of
       my service contract? 52

3.19 Will the shareholders have to approve any of the terms of my service
       contract? 52

3.20 Will my name appear on the company notepaper? 53

3.21 I've been asked by the company's bankers to give a guarantee
       of its bank overdraft. Should I? 53

Becoming a director

3.1   Am I eligible to be a director?

Almost anybody can be a company director. The law does not require any qualifications before a person can be made a director and, as any legal person can be a director, so can a company. There are the following exceptions to these general rules:

- Where the Articles of a company impose any special requirements for qualification or disqualification. For example, under the current Table A you will cease to be a director if:

    - You are prohibited by law and, in particular, the Companies Act 1985 from being a director.

    - You become bankrupt or make any arrangements or composition with your creditors.

    - You satisfy certain conditions relating to mental disorder.

    - You resign by notice.

    - You are absent from board meetings without the other directors' permission for more than six consecutive months and they resolve that your office be vacated.

- Where you have been disqualified from being a director by the courts (see chapter 13).

- You may not be made a director of a *public* company or of a *subsidiary* of a *public* company if you are 70 years old or more, unless your appointment is made or approved by the shareholders in general meeting when you reach the age of 70. Furthermore, if you are aware that you are being proposed for appointment or reappointment (say, by rotation) and you are over this age limit, you must give notice of this to the company.

3.2 How many directors should a company have?

This depends. The 1985 Act does not specify the maximum number of directors, but lays down the minimum number required. A private company has to have at least one director, but a sole director cannot also be the company secretary. A public company, on the other hand, must have at least two directors. The company's Articles of association will normally deal with the method of appointment of directors and fix the maximum and, subject to the 1985 Act, the minimum number.

3.3 What should I find out about a company before accepting appointment?

Clearly, your approach to accepting appointment as a director will depend on whether or not you are a stranger to the company. If you are already a senior manager of a company, you may have extensive knowledge of your company's affairs, although possibly only in respect of a limited part of it. If you are to be appointed from outside, or are asked to be a non-executive director of a company, you may have little or no knowledge of it. In either case, you are well advised to find out the role that would be expected of you and as much as you can about your company, in the light of the responsibilities you are to take on.

You should ask to be provided with information such as a written brief of what the job entails, a copy of the company's Memorandum and Articles and the latest audited financial statements.

Sources of information that are available to the general public and to which you may wish to refer include those noted below. Generally, these sources can be used to investigate 'standing' information (for example, addresses, trade names, markets served, number of employees, bankers and similar information) for a company or a group.

All information required to be filed by law can be obtained personally, or by using one of the many agencies specialising in obtaining such information. Companies House information is also available on line from the Companies House database (telephone 01222 381212 for companies registered in England and Wales or in Scotland)

Directory of Directors

This is an annual publication listing directors of major companies and identifying all directorships held by them.

Dun & Bradstreet

This is a major credit reference agency that will provide credit ratings as well as detailed information of use in assessing companies, including newspaper reports. The information is also maintained on a computer database. (Telephone 01494 422000)

Experian Limited (formerly CCN)

This company provides company information and credit reference checks. In addition to checks on companies, their database can check on directors to find out if they hold any other directorships and if there have been county court judgements against them – telephone (Nottingham) 0115 941 0888. Microfiches and company searches are available from Experian Business Information, telephone 0171 397 6711.

Financial Times Business Research Centre (formerly Extel)

This centre provides detailed financial information, primarily about listed companies and certain general information, on a card index or computer database. Also available on CD-ROM. (Telephone 0171 970 0211)

Key British Enterprises

This six volume book, published by Dun & Bradstreet, provides financial and basic information on the nature and size of companies' businesses, including products and services. It is also useful for identifying companies in similar businesses. Now available on CD-ROM.

Kompass

This two volume book published by Reed Business Information provides basic information on the nature and size of companies' businesses, including details of their products and services. It is also useful for identifying companies in similar businesses. Now also on a computer database. (Telephone 01342 326972)

Macmillan's Unquoted Companies

This two volume book provides summary financial information on the top 40,000 UK unquoted companies.

Stock Exchange Official Yearbook

This book contains a broad range of information relating to the Stock Exchange. It also contains information about listed companies and their directors. Available on CD-ROM with biographical information on directors taken from Who's Who in the City.

Reuters Business Briefing

This is computer database giving up-to-date information on companies from newspapers, journals, press releases, news reports, etc.

Who Owns Whom

This is a two volume book that is designed to help anyone wishing to identify relationships between companies. Also available on line and on CD-ROM. This is updated more frequently than the printed version.

The sources noted below will assist you to make comparisons between the results of a company and other companies in the same industrial sector or between a company and the industrial sector average.

Datastream

This on-line database maintains extensive information on a wide variety of matters of financial, business and economic interest. Information is mainly numeric and statistical rather than textual. For instance, accounts, directors, prices/dividends, and large shareholders in public companies.

Inter-Company-Comparisons (ICC)

This on line database is designed to provide information on, and facilitate comparisons between, over 1.2 million limited liability companies on the register of companies at Companies House. (Telephone 0181 783 1122; Internet address http:\\www.icc.co.uk).

In addition, useful information can be obtained from the financial press.

The areas that you should particularly address before accepting appointment as a director are:

- Whether the company is a going concern. This may be difficult to ascertain unless you have access to internal information. The most obvious place to look will be to see whether the financial statements are prepared on a going concern basis and to see whether the audit report is qualified. Otherwise, the basic consideration will be whether the company appears able to meet its debts as they fall due. Indications to the contrary will often include:

  - Recurring operating losses.

  - Significant amount of long overdue debts.

  - Particular susceptibility to a decline in consumer demand.

  - Heavy dependence on short–term finance for long-term needs.

- Shortage of working capital.

- Low liquidity ratios.

- High or increasing debt to equity gearing ratios.

- Under-capitalisation, in particular, a deficiency on share capital and reserves.

- Intra-group guarantees indicating a dependence on a holding company.

- Major contingent liabilities, for example, litigation over the right to produce the company's product.

None of these indications is ever conclusive, however, and you should look carefully at the positive aspects of a company as well; for example, the value of its assets and strength of its management.

- The integrity of the company's management.

- The company's position compared with its competitors.

- The detailed terms to be included in your service contract.

Before finally accepting the appointment as a director you might ask to be provided with all the management accounts from the date of the last audited financial statements, the most recent reports from the auditors to the board, and the board minutes for the last year. You might also ask to talk to the company's advisers.

3.4   Can I hold more than one directorship?

Yes. As an individual, you may hold any number of directorships you wish. Particulars of these other directorships must be included on Form 288 (Notice of change of directors or secretaries or in their particulars – see question 2.31) and filed with the Registrar.

It is likely where more than one directorship is held that some of these directorships will be non-executive (see question 3.12) and, therefore, that there may be no legal requirement for continuous attention to be given to the affairs of one company. However, if you are contemplating accepting appointment to a number of directorships, you should consider fully whether you have the time to deal with the affairs of each company. Otherwise, there is a risk that you will, through inadvertence, face disqualification (see chapter 13).

Furthermore, the more directorships you hold, the more likely you are to find yourself placed in a conflict of interest between competing companies. You are not prevented from being the director of a rival company. However, the courts are willing to restrain a director of one company, by injunction, from disclosing trade secrets or confidential information about one company to a rival company of which he is also a director.

3.5 I already do the same job as the other directors and attend board meetings. Am I in fact a director?

You may well be. Company law defines a director as including "*any person occupying the position of a director, by whatever name called*". The reason for this is that some companies (for example schools that operate as a company) prefer not to use the title 'director', but are managed in fact by a board of 'governors' or a 'management committee'. Where such individuals have the same function as a 'director', the law regards them as such. In your situation, you are unlikely to be regarded as a director unless, in addition, you actively take part in board meetings and vote at them. If you think you may be a director, however, you really ought to seek professional advice as you may risk being regarded as one.

3.6 I've been promoted to 'director of marketing'. I am a real director, aren't I?

As in the situation above, the answer to this question will depend on whether you occupy the position of a director, and not on your title. The risk is that if you do not sit on the board, you will not have access to the information you need to ascertain what the company's position really is. Yet you may still be treated as a director for legal purposes. It is sometimes thought that 'Director of ...' implies that the holder of the title does not sit on the board, while ' ... Director' is usually taken to imply that he does. However, the fact that your title contains the word 'director' must strongly imply that you *are* a director and that you would, therefore, have the responsibilities that go with that office.

The same considerations apply to anyone who is given what is termed an 'associate' directorship, which includes being called a 'regional', 'area' or 'divisional' director.

3.7 I've been asked to be an 'alternate director'. What does that mean?

What it means to be an 'alternate director' will depend upon the Articles of your company. If these are based on Table A your position will be as follows. Any director of your company has the power to appoint a person to be an alternate director and to remove that person. If the person that he wishes to appoint is not already a director (as will usually be the case) then the board must approve the appointment by resolution. Your appointment as an alternate director is dependent upon the person who appointed you remaining a director. If he ceases to be a director for any reason, you will cease to be an alternate director automatically. The only exception to this is where the director who appointed you ceases to be a director and is deemed reappointed (for example, where the Articles provide for retirement by rotation (see question 12.6)).

As an alternate director, you are regarded by the law as a full director of your company. Although the relationship between you and the director who appoints you may bear some similarities to that of principal and agent, this is not how the law regards it. In the absence of the director who appointed you, you will be entitled to do all that he can do. Therefore, you will, in the usual way, be entitled to notice of board meetings and notice of committee meetings where the appointing director is a member. However, you are entitled to attend and to vote at board meetings only when the director who appointed you is *absent*.

3.8 What are the formalities attached to being appointed an alternate director?

As noted above, company law regards an alternate director as a full director. Consequently, the appointment of an alternate director should be notified to the Registrar as a change of director on Form 288 (Notice of change of directors or secretaries or in their particulars). You would also have to be disclosed as a director in the company's annual financial statements and any remuneration you receive for your services as a director would have to be included in the disclosures of directors' emoluments in those financial statements.

Table A requires the appointment or removal of an alternate director to be notified to the company in writing signed by the director (or in some other manner approved by the directors).

3.9 I've been asked to be a 'nominee director'. What does that mean?

A 'nominee director' is usually understood to mean a director who is appointed to the board of a company on the 'nomination', that is, the request, of a party outside of that company. Common situations where such an appointment is made are:

- Where a joint venture company is set up by two companies and the Articles of the joint venture company or other agreement provide for the appointment of such directors.

- Where an investor in a company wishes to maintain some control over his investment.

The formalities for such an appointment are the same as those for the other categories of director discussed above. Equally, the powers and the responsibilities of a nominee director are the same as for other directors. This is particularly important to bear in mind if you are offered such an appointment. A director's duties are owed to his company. As discussed above, there is no prohibition on a director holding directorships of more than one company, *provided only* that this does not lead to any conflict of interest.

Where it does, as a nominee directorship frequently could, the individual director concerned would be at risk of being liable to the company that he was a nominee director of for any damage done. The full ramifications of this are considered in the Institute of Directors' booklet, *Nominee Directors*. It would make little difference in this context whether or not the director appointed as nominee was, in fact, a director of the nominating company or not, if such a conflict of interest could be shown.

Companies considering the appointment of a nominee to another company should also take into account the possibility of being regarded as a 'shadow director' of that company and the effect that might have upon them (see below).

3.10 I've heard of 'shadow directors'. What are they?

You can be a shadow director of a company without being formally appointed a director of it. All that the law requires is that the directors of a company are accustomed to act in accordance with your directions or instructions. The only exception to this rule is where the directors act on advice given by you in your professional capacity alone (for example, if you are the company's accountant). Therefore, if, for example, you own some shares in a company and the directors invariably do what you say, you will be a shadow director.

3.11 What are the implications of being a shadow director?

Many provisions of the Companies Act 1985 apply to shadow directors as well as to directors, so it is not possible to avoid liability by not being formally appointed a director if you come within the definition of shadow director. In addition, various provisions of the Insolvency Act 1986 are applied to shadow directors, in particular those relating to wrongful trading. Wrongful trading is dealt with fully in chapter 15. Also, some of the provisions of the Company Directors Disqualification Act 1986 are applied to shadow directors, in particular, the duty of the court to disqualify unfit directors of insolvent companies (see also chapter 13). So again it is not possible to avoid liability purely by not being appointed a director.

3.12 I've been asked to be a 'non-executive director' of a company. What does this entail?

An executive director is usually an employee of a company and has an executive function within it. A non-executive director will not be an employee of the company and will frequently be appointed on a part-time basis only.

However, you should ensure that you will have the time not only to attend board meetings, but also to do such reading and preparation as is necessary to keep informed about the business activities of the company in particular and the industry in which your company is involved in general.

You, as a non-executive director, will be expected to show the same duty of care and fiduciary duty to your company as an executive director (see question 5.2). A non-executive director will also be subject to the same liability as any other director in relation to compensating their company for loss arising from breaches by directors of their duties and also in relation to disqualification. Because of this, you should ensure that you have the same access to information within the company as other directors have.

In fact, the Institute of Directors in its booklet, *Guidelines for Directors* paragraph 84 advises that even private companies, large or small, that wish to maintain an active control over their future, can benefit from the appointment of suitable non-executive directors. The Institute also assesses what the proper contribution of non-executive directors is by saying *"The overriding consideration is that they participate to the full in the board's joint deliberations. Their legal duty to act* bona fide *in the interests of the company as a whole is identical with that of their executive colleagues"*. The Institute goes on to describe the three further contributions their independence has to make. These can be summarised as:

- To widen the horizons within which the board determines strategy by bringing relevant wider general or special experience into board discussions;

- To take responsibility for monitoring management performance and the extent to which management is achieving the results planned when the strategy was determined.

■ To ensure the board has adequate systems to safeguard the interests of the company where these may conflict with the personal interest of directors: to exercise a duty in such areas as board appointments and remuneration: and to ensure the presentation of adequate financial information, whether or not an audit committee exists.

If you, as a non-executive director, consider that insufficient financial information is available to the board, it is your duty to bring it to the board's attention of the board. You should, therefore, read carefully chapter 5 of this book dealing with a director's duties to his company.

Non-executive directors of listed companies may be asked to sit on certain board committees the company should set up, for instance the nomination committee. Unless the board of a listed company is small, a nomination committee should be established under the Combined Code to make recommendations to the board on all new board appointments. It is a principle of the Code that there should be a formal and transparent procedure for the appointment of new directors to the board.

3.13 I've heard some non-executive directors are called independent. Is this distinction important?

This distinction is now generally recognised as being important. The requirement for independent non-executives to be appointed to the board of a listed company forms part of the recommendations of the Cadbury and Hampel Reports. In addition, the Combined Code sets out the following as a principle of good governance.

> *"The board should include a balance of executive and non-executive directors (including independent non-executives) such that no individual or small group of individuals can dominate the board's decision taking."*

This is supplemented by the Combined Code's best practice provisions that non-executives should comprise not less than one third of the board. Furthermore, under these provisions the majority of the non-executives of listed companies should be independent of management and free from any business or other relationship that could materially interfere with the exercise of their independent judgment. The Cadbury Committee's recommendation for boards to have at least three non-executive directors, of which two must be independent, has been relaxed in favour of these more flexible requirements.

Independent non-executive directors of listed companies are likely to sit on their company's remuneration and audit committees as well as nomination committees. Under the best practice provisions of the Combined Code, boards of listed companies should set up remuneration committees made up exclusively of independent non-executive directors to avoid potential conflicts of interest in setting remuneration packages for the executive directors. The Combined Code also says that audit committees of at least three non-executive directors (the majority of which should be independent) should be set up. A company which is listed on the Stock Exchange must include in its financial statements a statement of the identity of the independent non-executive directors together with a short biographical note on each.

3.14 Are there any formalities on being appointed a director?

Yes. If you are to be a director when a company is first formed, you will need to be named on Form 10 (Statement of first directors and secretary and intended situation of registered office). This should give details of your full name and address, business occupation, nationality, date of birth, and any other directorships you may hold. You must sign the form to indicate that you consent to act as a director of the company. The form must be sent to the Registrar at the same time as the proposed company's Memorandum of Association. The requirement to register directors' other directorships is likely to be abolished in the near future.

If you are being appointed a director of an existing company, a Form 288a or 288ab(I) will need to be completed. The information to be given is similar to that required by Form 10 above, but must additionally state the date of appointment. You must also sign the form to indicate that you consent to act as a director. The Form must be sent to the Registrar within 14 days of the change.

If the company is listed on the Stock Exchange, the appointment must be notified immediately to the Stock Exchange. A new director may be required to submit a detailed declaration as well. Furthermore, any important change in the holding of an executive office must be notified to the Stock Exchange Company Announcements Office.

In addition, the appointment of a director must always be recorded in the company's own Register of Directors and Secretaries. The details to be recorded are the same as required on Forms 10 and 288a. Any changes in the particulars (including any change of address) must be notified within 14 days to the Registrar on Form 288c or 288c(I).

3.15 If I become a director of a company will I be one of its employees?

This will depend upon the nature of your appointment. If you are an executive director you will invariably be an employee as well. However, non-executive directors are not employees and should have no contractual relationship with the board, other than that relating to the office as a director, in order to maintain independence. One example of the effects of the distinction is that you will receive a salary as an employee, but fees as a director. In many cases, however, an executive director's fees will be included in his management salary.

3.16 Should I have a service contract with my company?

If you are an executive director then you are likely to be an employee of the company. Your terms of employment will be contained in your service contract with the company. Basic particulars of the terms of your employment must be given to you in a written statement so as to satisfy the requirements of the Employment Rights Act 1996, which is the situation with all employees. However, it is usual for an executive director to have a full written service contract with his employing company, which deals with his rights and responsibilities to the company and *vice versa*.

3.17 What terms should be included in my service contract?

The specific terms of your service contract will depend on your particular circumstances and those of your company. Consequently, it is never wise to make use of any 'model' service contract without taking professional advice on whether it needs to be amended. However, you should not be surprised to see terms with the following effect:

- That your duties and powers will be those that the board may from time to time properly assign to you in connection with the company's business.

- That you must comply with the board's proper and reasonable decisions.

- That you must devote the whole of your time and attention to your company's business. This may be combined with a provision that you will not undertake any other occupation whilst being a director of the company.

- That any intellectual property discovered or made by you during the course of your employment, which is capable of being used in the company's business, will be the company's property.

- That you will treat as confidential any information that you obtain because of your position within the company both whilst a director and thereafter.

- That you will not compete with the company on termination of your employment. To be enforceable this will usually be limited to specific activities, a defined period of time and a precise geographical area.

In addition, the service contract will contain clauses dealing with:

- Your remuneration and benefits.
- Whether there is a company pension scheme you can join.
- Any compensation you are entitled to for loss of office.
- How your service contract may be terminated.
- The period of duration of your service contract. (Note, this may need approval by the company's shareholders. This is discussed in question 3.19)

3.18 Will the shareholders be able to see any of the terms of my service contract?

Yes. A company must keep a copy of all directors' service contracts with the company and its subsidiaries at the company's registered office, its principal place of business, or where it maintains its Register of Members. If there is no written service contract, a written memorandum of the terms on which directors serve must be kept. In either situation, all changes in the terms of the contract made since it was entered into must be shown. However, your company need not keep any copy or memorandum of your contract if it has less than a year to run or can be terminated within a year without compensation.

Your company does not have to keep a copy of your contract if it requires you to work wholly or mainly outside the UK. Instead, it must keep a memorandum showing your name and the duration of the contract. Where your contract is with a subsidiary company, the memorandum must give the name of that company.

Your company must notify the Registrar of where the copies or memoranda are kept, unless they are kept at the registered office. Shareholders may inspect them free of charge. If inspection is refused the shareholder can go to court and get an order for inspection to be allowed.

3.19 Will the shareholders have to approve any of the terms of my service contract?

In general, no. However, if you want your contract to include a term requiring your company or any of its subsidiaries to employ you for more than five years, during which period your employment cannot be terminated, then that term must be approved *beforehand* by ordinary resolution of the shareholders in a general meeting (see chapter 8). The law contains complicated provisions to deal with variations on this theme, for example, to cover the situation where you may already be employed under such a contract before appointment as a director.

Where shareholders' approval is required, a written memorandum setting out the *whole* of the proposed contract must be made available for the shareholders to inspect for 15 days before that meeting and at the meeting itself. Should your contract inadvertently have been entered into without such approval, it will still be valid. However, the term providing for its duration will not be valid. The law then 'deems' your contract to include a term entitling the company to terminate your contract on giving reasonable notice. What is meant by 'reasonable' is not defined. It is unlikely, however, to exceed three months.

However, corporate governance considers it best practice to have directors' service contracts which last for significantly shorter periods. Although the law permits contract periods of up to five years without the shareholders' approval, the Cadbury Committee's Code of Best Practice recommended that the service contracts of directors of UK listed companies should not exceed *three* years without shareholders' approval. The Combined Code best practice provisions state that there is a strong case for setting contract periods at, or reducing them to, one year or less. These measures are basically aimed at restricting the amount of the termination payment a director can receive, without shareholder approval, where his contract is terminated before the end of the contract period.

3.20 Will my name appear on the company notepaper?

There is no longer any legal requirement that the names of a company's directors should appear on its business correspondence. However, where a company incorporated on or after 23 November 1916 states the name of *any* director on its business correspondence, it must go on to state clearly the surname and Christian name or other forename (or initials) of *all* its directors. Where a director is a company, its corporate name must be given.

3.21 I've been asked by the company's bankers to give a guarantee of its bank overdraft. Should I?

Frequently, a personal guarantee will be the only way of the company obtaining finance, particularly when an existing business is incorporated for the first time. However, there is always a risk that if your business is unsuccessful your company may become insolvent. In this event you will be liable on the guarantee you have given. Furthermore, such a guarantee may involve the bankers taking a charge over your family home, which you could risk losing if the guarantee were to be enforced.

You should always give very careful consideration to the risks entailed in giving a personal guarantee. You should see your solicitor and ask him to run through the terms of the guarantee with you, for example, the extent and duration of the guarantee and how and when it can be enforced. You should see your accountant to discuss with him the future prospects of your business (and, in particular, its cash requirements), and hence whether the finance you have obtained is likely to prove to be adequate.

Your functions as a director

Question   *Page*

4.1   What powers do I have as a director? 57

4.2   Can I delegate any of my powers? 58

4.3   When can I enter into contracts on my company's behalf? 58

4.4   Should I sign contracts in my own name or in the company's? ... 58

4.5   Should I sign all cheques? 59

4.6   Am I entitled to look at any of the company's records? 59

4.7   Can I appoint someone to act in my place, say, if I will be abroad for a few months? 60

4.8   How far can I trust what my employees do without checking their work myself? 60

4.9   What safeguards should I introduce? 61

4.10 I've been asked to be the company's 'Managing Director'. What does that entail? 61

4.11 Are there any formalities to being appointed a Managing Director? 62

Chapter 4

Your functions as a director

4.1 What powers do I have as a director?

The Articles of your company will describe a great many powers that relate to the management of the company. They will generally provide that the business of the company is to be managed by the directors. See Table A, regulation 70. However, they will probably not make clear the position of individual directors. The variety of structures adopted in practice for company boards makes it unlikely that any standard set of rules applicable to all directors could be devised (for example, because of the distinction between executive and non-executive directors). Table A permits the board to appoint a managing director or other executive directors and to delegate its powers on any basis it chooses to a committee. Since a committee can be represented by a single director then the board may delegate any of its powers to that director.

You should ensure that you are aware of the limits of the powers delegated to you by the board. This means that you will know what transactions you may enter into on behalf of the company without first obtaining a resolution of the board authorising you to enter into them. The best practice provisions of the Combined Code acknowledge that the board of directors of a company should have a formal schedule of matters specifically reserved to it for decision.

As a member of the board, you have a responsibility to see that it manages the company's business effectively and plays its part in corporate governance. A principle of the Combined Code is that every listed company should be headed by an effective board, which should lead and control the company.

4.2 Can I delegate any of my powers?

There seems to be no reason why not as this is usually permitted by a company's Articles. However, where you do delegate any of your powers, as a director you still remain responsible for their exercise and will still have a duty of care to your company. (See question 5.2). Therefore, it is always good practice to confirm what you are delegating in writing to the manager or other members of staff concerned.

4.3 When can I enter into contracts on my company's behalf?

You can bind the company to any contract which would normally be within the powers of a director of your type. If you are a Managing Director you can bind the company to any contract that is in the ordinary course of your company's business. Your company will be bound even if you have not been delegated power to enter that type of contract by your board. This stems from the legal rule laid down in the case of *Royal British Bank v. Turquand [1856]* 6 E&B 327 that a person dealing with a company in good faith is entitled, in the absence of some indication to the contrary, to assume that the company has complied with all matters of internal procedure necessary for it to enter a valid contract. If a contract is outside the authority delegated to you by the board, it is advisable for the board by resolution to approve the contract and your signature on behalf of the company before you sign. However, the contract should in any case still be within the *company's* capacity to enter into as defined by its objects clause (see question 2.3), and within the powers of the directors as set out in the Articles.

4.4 Should I sign contracts in my own name or in the company's?

When you enter into a contract on your company's behalf, you are acting as its agent. It is important, therefore, that this agency is clearly established or otherwise you will risk being personally liable on the contract. Usually it is sufficient if you sign 'for and on behalf of' your company, particularly if the context makes it clear that you intended to contract as agent of your company. It will help in making this clear if you carry out all correspondence on your company's headed letter paper and also if you sign as 'Mr X, Director' or as appropriate. Where large or unusual contracts are concerned you would be wise to take professional advice.

4.5 Should I sign all cheques?

This will depend upon whose names are on the bank mandate. Commonly, this may be the directors only, particularly where the company has grown quickly from being owned/managed by the directors. Usually, it is possible for an arrangement to be made with your company's bank, whereby specified individuals can be delegated responsibility for signing cheques up to a certain amount. Alternatively, mechanical cheque signing arrangements can be devised or sophisticated funds transfer systems could be introduced where the volume of cheques is substantial. In a large company it may not be appropriate for a director to sign all cheques or payment authorisations relating to his area of responsibility. It is also better management to delegate responsibility down the chain of command as far as is practicable, provided that, in this instance, suitable controls over the cheque signatories and payment authorisations are introduced.

One matter you should be careful of is that the company name is accurately described on any cheque or order and includes at the end of the name 'limited' in the case of a private company or, in the case of a public company, 'public limited company', or their permitted abbreviations, 'ltd.' or 'plc' respectively. Companies whose registered office is in Wales may use the Welsh equivalents. If the name is not accurately described you will not only be personally liable on the cheque if the company does not honour it, but also you will be personally liable on summary conviction to a maximum fine of £1,000.

4.6 Am I entitled to look at any of the company's records?

As a director, you have a statutory right to inspect your company's accounting records and case law makes it clear that you may inspect the company's statutory books. You should be able to inspect and take copies of any document you need to carry out your own duties, or that are relevant to ascertaining whether any statutory obligation has been fulfilled that you as a company officer could be liable for if breached. If a matter does concern you, the appropriate forum to raise it is at a board meeting. The duty of directors to ensure that proper accounting records are kept is dealt with in question 7.6.

4.7 Can I appoint someone to act in my place, say, if I will be abroad for a few months?

Yes. You can appoint an 'alternate' director (see question 3.8).

4.8 How far can I trust what my employees do without checking their work myself?

The extent of your duties is considered in chapter 5. The basic proposition in respect of this question is that:

> *"In respect of all duties that, having regard to the exigencies of business, and the Articles of association, may properly be left to some other official, a director is, in the absence of grounds for suspicion, justified in trusting that official to perform such duties honestly."* [Re City Equitable Fire Insurance Co. Ltd [1925] Ch 407]

This has been stated in another case, where Lord Halsbury LC said in relation to the directors of a bank:

> *"I cannot think that it can be expected of a director that he should be watching either the inferior officers of the bank or verifying the calculations of the auditors himself. The business of life could not go on if people could not trust those who are put into a position of trust for the express purpose of attending to details of management."* [Davey v. Cary [1901] AC 477].

You should bear in mind, however, that if you are in an executive role, a court is more likely now to find that you had grounds for suspicion or were negligent in trusting a particular official than in earlier cases. This is because these cases date back to the turn of the century, and reflect the different appreciation of a director's role and responsibilities that prevailed at that time. It is now clear that directors must put in place certain controls to safeguard shareholders' investment and the company's assets.

4.9 What safeguards should I introduce?

It is recommended that a system is introduced to ensure that there is effective control over the actions of company officials. The establishment and maintenance of proper internal controls to cover this and other areas, such as the maintenance of proper accounting records, is now considered a key aspect of the efficient management of a company. Directors of larger companies may wish to think about setting up an internal audit department (see question 7.16).

The Hampel Report recommended that directors should maintain and review the internal controls addressing all relevant control objectives. It said that these should include business risk assessment and response, financial management, compliance with laws and regulations and the safeguarding of assets, including minimising the risk of fraud. It is a principle of the Combined Code that directors of listed companies should conduct a review at least annually of the effectiveness of the group's system of internal controls and report to shareholders that they have done so. This review should cover all controls, including financial, operational and compliance controls and risk management.

4.10 I've been asked to be the company's 'Managing Director'. What does that entail?

Precisely what powers you will have as a Managing Director will depend on the powers delegated to you by your board or given to you in your service contract. People outside the company can assume that you have the power to enter into contracts of *any type* on your company's behalf. Hence, you will in general be able to bind your company in respect of contracts of any type. This is in contrast to the position of, for example, a Finance Director, who can bind his company only in respect of those contracts which it is normal for a Finance Director to enter into.

In addition, under Table A a Managing Director is not required to retire by rotation (see question 12.6)

4.11 Are there any formalities to being appointed a Managing Director?

First, the Articles of your company must specifically entitle the board to delegate its powers to a Managing Director. Table A does so.

Secondly, you must be formally appointed by the board. The powers to be delegated to you should be specifically approved and the fact of your appointment must be noted in the board minutes.

Chapter 5

Your duties as a director to your company

Question   *Page*

5.1   Why do directors have a duty to their company? 65

5.2   To whom am I responsible as a director? 65
        Your duty of care 66
        Your fiduciary duties 67
        Your duty to act within your powers 68

5.3   I am a director of a subsidiary company. Do these duties
        still apply? 69

5.4   I know that my company is about to enter into a contract
        with a company in which I own shares.
        Do I need to do anything? 69

5.5   Can I get around this by entering into an arrangement with the
        company I own rather than a legally binding contract? 69

5.6   When do I have to disclose my interest? 70

5.7   Can I vote on a contract in which I have declared an interest? . . . 70

5.8   My company enters into a large number of such contracts.
        Do I have to go through this procedure every time? 71

5.9   What happens if I don't disclose my interest in a contract? 71

5.10 Will only the board know of such contracts? 71

5.11 Is that all? 71

5.12 What happens if these procedures are not followed? 72

5.13 I am a director of a listed company. Are there any additional
requirements I must satisfy? 72
AIM Companies 73

5.14 Can I use the company's assets for my own benefit? 74

5.15 My company has had to turn down a contract because it has
too much work. Can I take it on personally? 74

5.16 Can my company give to my favourite charity? 74

5.17 Can my company exempt me from or indemnify me against
any liability I incur as a director? 75

5.18 Can I insure against being liable as a director? 75

5.19 The words 'summary trial' and 'trial on indictment' are
used to describe offences under the Companies Act 1985.
What do they mean? 76

Chapter 5

Your duties as a director to your company

5.1   Why do directors have a duty to their company?

The duties that the law imposes on directors have developed because a director's relationship with his company is seen to be similar to other legal relationships (such as agency and trusteeship) which give rise to duties. In fact, you will be deemed a director, whether or not you are called a director, if you occupy the position of director. In some ways directors are seen as agents of their company as they can only act within the authority given to them by the Articles of association in the transactions they carry out on the company's behalf. In addition, directors are in some senses trustees (or fiduciaries) of the company's assets in that the property in their hands or under their control must be applied for the company's specific purpose. This fiduciary relationship imposes on directors duties of loyalty and good faith and, as agents, directors have the duties of care and skill to the company (which is their principal).

5.2   To whom am I responsible as a director?

As has been mentioned above, directors, by virtue of their relationship with the company, owe certain duties to the company. These are general duties, applicable in all circumstances, arising under the common law, from the relationship between the directors and the company and they are owed by each director individually. In addition, Parliament has laid down specific duties that company directors owe to their company. These are considered later in this chapter. The three general duties are considered below. First, a director has 'a duty of care'. This is concerned with the degree of care, diligence and skill that a company director is required to exercise in order not to be considered to have done his legitimate duties badly. Secondly, he has 'fiduciary duties'. This includes a duty to act *bona fide* in the interests of his company, thus restricting the acts that a director can properly do in connection with the management of the company. Thirdly, he has a strict duty to act only within his powers as a director.

Your duty of care

This is the first duty. The traditional view of the standard of care that a director is expected to show to his company gives the impression that this duty is not very onerous. However, the duty to show care has been shown not to be so limited as once thought.

At present the law does not state clearly what the standard of care is that a director must show. However, it is thought that the higher courts would uphold the following standard of care. This is that a director is required to act as a reasonably diligent person having not only the same general knowledge and experience as the director, but also the general knowledge and skill to be expected of a person having the same functions. This is similar to the rest applied on section 214 of the Insolvency Act 1986 (see question 15.4).

The case of *Dorchester Finance Co. Ltd and another v. Stebbing and others* [1989] BCLC 498 showed that no distinction is to be drawn between executive and non-executive directors.

The facts of that case were that P and H were non-executive directors who left management of the company's affairs to a third director, S. S and P were chartered accountants and H had accounting experience. P and H rarely visited the company's head office and no board meetings were held. They often signed cheques in blank to be signed by S at some later date and made no attempt to ascertain how the funds acquired from the parent company were used by S. P and H took no part in its business and both alleged that they had relied on the auditors and the fact that the relevant financial statements were not qualified. The judge concluded that not only had P and H failed to exhibit the necessary skill and care in the performance of their duties as directors, but they had failed to perform any duty at all as directors of the company. He also found that S failed to exercise any skill or care as a director and that he knowingly misapplied the company's assets. They were all liable for damages.

It is clear from this case that, whether you are an executive or a non-executive director, you must take the duty of care you owe as a director seriously. If you do not, and are in breach of it, it may not be a defence to say that you did not take part in management or relied on others. For instance, you may be considered to be negligent if you do not attend board meetings regularly or do not ensure that you are kept sufficiently informed about the company's assets and financial position.

Your fiduciary duties

Directors must act *"bona fide in what they consider – not what a court may consider – is in the interests of the company, and not for any collateral purpose"*. [Lord Greene in *Re Smith and Fawcett Ltd* [1942] Ch 304]. Company, in this context, is defined by reference to its shareholders as a whole (present and future) and not as a body that is distinct from its shareholders. This is to be compared with the fact that directors owe their duties to the company and not to individual shareholders. In addition, the duty to act *bona fide* in the best interests of the company is a subjective one. So long as the directors have correctly informed themselves as to what is meant by 'the company' in this context, it is left to them to decide where its best interests lie. The courts will interfere only if no reasonable director could possibly have concluded that a particular transaction was in the best interest of the company. Directors can be in breach of this duty without any conscious dishonesty on their part.

To be regarded as acting *bona fide* in the interests of your company, you may have to balance the different interests of the company, of different classes of current shareholders and of present and future shareholders.

You will, however, also now have to consider certain other factors. Directors have been given a statutory duty by the Companies Act 1985 to consider the interests of employees in general. Directors may, as a result of a statutory provision, have to consider the interests of customers or the general public, for instance, where safety or product liability matters are involved. As a consequence of the wrongful trading provisions of the Insolvency Act 1986 (see paragraph 15.4) directors may have to have regard to the interests of the company's creditors before those of shareholders if they are aware that there is no reasonable prospect that the company would avoid going into insolvent liquidation.

It can be seen that directors have several, possibly conflicting, interests to consider, and it is possible that they may offend the interests of one section while carrying out their duty to another. If this is the case they may be able to rely on the relief available under section 727 of the Companies Act 1985 if they acted honestly, reasonably and the court considers they ought fairly to be excused.

You must also make sure you do not place yourself in a position where your personal interests are liable to conflict with your duties to your company. If you do, you will be required to account for any benefit you receive, unless the shareholders have given consent or consent is given in the Articles.

Your duty to act within your powers

The third duty as a director is that you must not do anything that is outside the capacity of your company as laid down in the Memorandum of Association (see question 2.3). Under section 35 of the Companies Act 1985, it may be possible for the shareholders to ratify by special resolution an act that is not permitted by the Memorandum. However, a separate special resolution is required if, in addition to ratification of the act, the directors concerned are to be relieved from liability for that act.

Nor should you do anything that goes beyond the powers conferred upon you as a director by your company's Articles (see question 2.4) unless the shareholders expressly approve it, or will subsequently ratify it. If you do an act that is not permitted by the Articles, you will be in breach of your duties to the company and it would be entitled to recover the amount of its loss from you. In addition, the act may not bind the company and you may also be personally liable to the third party.

However, some acts cannot be ratified. These include:

- Acts involving a fraud on the minority.
- Fraudulent or dishonest acts.

■ Acts for which a special procedure is required and that procedure is not followed. For example, if no special resolution or court order is obtained before returning capital to shareholders, a transaction that amounts to an unauthorised return of capital cannot subsequently be ratified even if all shareholders agree.

5.3 I am a director of a subsidiary company. Do these duties still apply?

Your duties are to the company of which you are a director. If your company's parent company is accustomed to tell your board what to do, you and your fellow board members may sometimes find yourselves with conflicting interests. Unless you can, honestly and reasonably, come to the conclusion that the parent company's instructions are in the best interests of your company, you may be in breach of your duties if you follow them. If you are in any doubt you should take legal advice.

5.4 I know that my company is about to enter into a contract with a company in which I own shares. Do I need to do anything?

As a director, you must disclose to the board the nature of any direct or indirect interest you or a person connected with you (as defined later in question 10.1) have in *any* contract or proposed contract with your company (see below).

You will also be treated as being interested in any loans your company makes to you or a person connected with you and you should disclose your interest in such transactions.

5.5 Can I get around this by entering into an arrangement with the company I own rather than a legally binding contract?

No. Those who drafted the legislation foresaw this possibility and 'contract' includes, for this purpose, any transaction or arrangement, whether or not constituting a contract.

5.6   When do I have to disclose my interest?

As soon as a contract is proposed, the Companies Act 1985 requires that you should declare the nature of your interest at the first board meeting where the question of entering into the contract is considered. Where your interest arises only after a contract has been proposed or made, you should declare your interest at the next board meeting, whether or not that contract is to be considered.

The board of directors should ensure that by entering into the transaction they do not exceed any limitation on their powers under the company's constitution. If they do exceed any limitation, any director who authorised the transaction may be personally liable to the company for any loss. The transaction may also be avoided by the company unless ratified by the shareholders.

5.7   Can I vote on a contract in which I have declared an interest?

The new Table A does not prohibit you from voting provided that your interest is not material and does not conflict with the company's interests. However, it is probably best practice if you do not. If your company adopted the old Table A and has not amended it, you are prohibited from voting in respect of any contract or arrangement in which you are 'interested'. Furthermore, your vote (if you attempt to exercise it) must not be counted and your presence does not count towards the *quorum* for the meeting (see question 6.2).

There are limited exceptions to these provisions; for instance, where your interest arises only because you are to guarantee an obligation of the company or are to subscribe for shares in it. In any event, the old Table A provides that your company's shareholders in a general meeting can at any time suspend or relax the prohibition *generally* or in respect of any particular contract.

It is very common for companies to adopt their own provisions in respect of directors' interests in contracts and you should check the particular Articles of your company.

5.8 My company enters into a large number of such contracts. Do I have to go through this procedure every time?

No. You can give a general notice to the board either to the effect that:

■ you are a member of a specified company or firm and you are to be regarded as interested in any contract that may, after the date of the notice, be made with that company or firm; or

■ you are to be regarded as interested in any contract that may, after the date of the notice, be made with a connected person (as defined later in question 10.1).

5.9 What happens if I don't disclose my interest in a contract?

First, you are liable to be fined. On trial on indictment the fine is unlimited – on summary trial it is limited to a maximum of £5,000. Secondly, a court might subsequently take the view that entering into the contract was in breach of your fiduciary duty to your company (see question 5.2).

5.10 Will only the board know of such contracts?

If you have a material interest in a contract it will have to be disclosed in your company's financial statements. It is for the board to decide on whether a transaction is material or not. The details of what disclosures are required are considered from question 10.13.

5.11 Is that all?

No. There are further legal restrictions upon a company entering into what are called 'substantial property transactions' involving a director, who for this purpose includes the persons connected with him.

A company is prohibited from entering into an 'arrangement' with a director to acquire from, or transfer to, the company a non-cash asset, except where one of the following applies:

■ The shareholders approve it in advance in general meeting.

- The shareholders affirm it within a reasonable period.

- The value of the non-cash asset is less than £2,000 or, if it is greater, the lower of £100,000 or 10 per cent of the company's net assets.

- It is between a wholly-owned subsidiary and either its holding company or a fellow wholly-owned subsidiary.

- It is with a company that is being wound up (except by a members' voluntary winding up).

- The director is acquiring a non-cash asset in his capacity as a member of the company.

5.12 What happens if these procedures are not followed?

The company is entitled to treat the arrangement as void, unless one of the following applies:

- It is no longer possible for the cash or property involved to be restored to the company.

- A third party has in good faith given value to acquire rights that would be affected.

Furthermore, in this type of situation, you will be liable to account to the company for any gain you may have made as a result and to indemnify the company for any loss or damage it may suffer.

5.13 I am a director of a listed company. Are there any additional requirements I must satisfy?

Yes. These are contained in Chapter 11 of the Stock Exchange's Listing Rules. These set out the rules that companies applying to be listed on the Stock Exchange must follow in making their application and various continuing obligations that they are required to observe after listing. The Listing Rules require certain procedures to be complied with where a listed company (or any of its subsidiaries) proposes to enter into transactions with related parties.

Transactions with related parties include transactions (other than of a revenue nature in the ordinary course of business) between a company or a subsidiary and a director, or associate of his. 'Associate' in this respect includes the director's spouse and child and a company where he and his family control 30 per cent or more of the voting rights.

When a transaction with a related party is proposed the company must immediately notify the Company's Announcement Office giving details of the transaction. It must also send a circular to shareholders and obtain the approval of the company in general meeting before the transaction is entered into. The related party should not be allowed to vote at that meeting. Any circular sent to shareholders in this connection must provide sufficient information to enable any recipient of the circular to evaluate the effects of the transaction on the company. The ideal approach will generally involve an arithmetical evaluation being included in the circular.

However, certain transactions are excepted from the requirements mentioned above. These include small transactions. A small transaction is one where certain percentage ratios are not more than 0.25 per cent; for instance, the net assets of the transaction divided by the net assets of the listed company. Where transactions are larger than this, some disclosure will be necessary. Thus, if the percentage ratios of a transaction exceed 0.25 per cent but are less than five per cent, the company must give certain information to the Stock Exchange and include details of the transaction in its next annual financial statements. If the percentage ratios are five per cent or more, the requirements mentioned in the preceding paragraph will need to be satisfied. A company should consult the Stock Exchange at an early stage if there is any doubt as to whether and to what extent Chapter 11 of the Listing Rules applies.

AIM Companies

An AIM company that wishes to enter into a transaction with a related party must comply with the AIM Admission Rules. Details of any transaction between an AIM company and a related party where any of the specified ratios is five per cent or more must be notified to the Stock Exchange. The notification must include a statement by the directors that the terms of the transaction are fair and reasonable so far as the shareholders are concerned. If any of the percentage ratios is 0.25 per cent or more, details must also be included in the AIM company's next annual consolidated financial statements.

5.14 Can I use the company's assets for my own benefit?

A director has a duty not to profit personally from the use of his company's assets, information or opportunities. However, this will not apply if the shareholders have approved the transaction at a general meeting or it is permitted under the company's Articles of association. You cannot, in the absence of such approval, use the company's assets for your own benefit or to make a secret profit. If you do, you may be liable to the company for its loss or any profit you make.

5.15 My company has had to turn down a contract because it has too much work. Can I take it on personally?

Yes. However, you may only do so if you fully disclose all the information that is relevant about the contract to your board first. If the board, in good faith, decides to turn down the opportunity, you may take the contract on personally, provided that no term of your service contract prohibits this. It is recommended in such circumstances that the board minutes its reasons for rejecting the opportunity, to show that it was done in good faith, just in case this was to be challenged at a later date. One example where the decision could be in good faith is where the company cannot do the work itself.

5.16 Can my company give to my favourite charity?

If your company has made good profits during a year, you and your fellow directors may wish to benefit the community or the less fortunate by making a donation out of these profits to a charity. However, this will generally not be possible unless your company's Memorandum of association permits the company to make such gifts. This is because, in the absence such authority, you can only use the company's assets for its benefit. It would normally be unlikely that a donation by the company to a charity would be for its obvious benefit. Thus, before you make a charitable donation you may need to ensure that your company's Memorandum permits the donation or the shareholders have approved it. Otherwise you may be in breach of your duty to act in the company's interests.

In addition, the amount of each charitable donation over £200 that a company makes in a financial year and the purposes for which it was made must be disclosed in the Directors' Report for the year.

5.17 Can my company exempt me from or indemnify me against any liability I incur as a director?

Your company cannot alter its Articles, or put a term in your service contract, so as to exempt you from or indemnify you against any liability you may suffer for negligence, breach of duty or breach of trust that you may commit against it. The law provides that any such term would be void. The only exceptions to this are that your company can agree to indemnify you in respect of the costs of defending civil or criminal proceedings that you win and can purchase or maintain insurance against such liabilities.

5.18 Can I insure against being liable as a director?

You can insure against most forms of civil action that may be taken against you. In fact, this is increasingly common in practice. It should be remembered that even though you have insurance cover, your duties and obligations to your company will still be the same. Also, bear in mind that some forms of civil action, such as for libel and slander, and all forms of criminal proceedings, will usually be uninsurable.

Because of an amendment to section 310 of the Companies Act 1985, it is now possible for a company to take out and pay for directors and officers liability insurance indemnifying its directors against liability arising from acts comprising negligence, default, breach of duty or trust committed by the directors whilst performing their duties as directors. As a rule, policies will cover wrongful acts such as breach of trust, breach of duty, neglect and misstatement, but will exclude liability in a number of cases, including claims arising from dishonesty, fraud, slander, libel, pollution, breach of professional duty and claims based on the director gaining a profit or advantage to which he was not legally entitled.

However, you should check the company's Memorandum and Articles before the company takes out such insurance, to ensure it is within the company's objects and the directors' powers to do so. The fact that the company has purchased such insurance need no longer be mentioned in the directors' report. You will, however, need to take advice as to whether payment of the premium by the company will be taxable as a benefit to you.

Where a company has decided not to provide such cover, it may still be possible for a director to obtain cover on an individual basis. Your professional advisers will be able to give you help in this matter.

Despite the cost, it is recommended that companies take out such insurance. Even a relatively small claim, in commercial terms, can be ruinous if it has to be borne personally by a director (not least because of the associated legal costs).

5.19   The words 'summary trial' and 'trial on indictment' are used to describe offences under the Companies Act 1985. What do they mean?

In legal terms, the words 'summary trial' or 'summary conviction' and the expression 'trial on indictment' are used in connection with criminal offences to indicate the mode of trial. Summary trial takes place in a court of summary jurisdiction, which is a court where justices of the peace or other magistrates sit. The offences tried this way are called summary offences and are generally the less serious offences. Some offences, however, are triable either as summary offences or as indictable offences. In this event, if the magistrates consider that the circumstances or nature of the case make the offence one of a serious character, or that the punishment they have power to inflict would not be adequate, they may refer the offence for trial on indictment in the Crown Court where the accused will be tried by a jury.

Chapter 6

Your duties to your co-directors

Question   *Page*

6.1   Do directors need to hold regular board meetings? 79

6.2   How many directors need to attend a board meeting? 79

6.3   Where should a board meeting be held? 80

6.4   What notice should be given beforehand? 81

6.5   Who should be given notice? 81

6.6   What should the notice contain? 82

6.7   Should there be a chairman of a board meeting? 82

6.8   What questions need to be dealt with at a board meeting? 83

6.9   What majority is needed for board decisions? 83

6.10 Must I attend board meetings? 84

6.11 Can I be excluded from any board meeting? 84

6.12 The directors of our company are spread throughout the UK and
      some abroad. Can we avoid having a formal board meeting? 85

6.13 We seem to cover a lot of routine business at board meetings.
      Can we appoint committees to deal with these matters? 85

6.14 Do minutes of board meetings need to be taken? 86

6.15 What should be recorded in the minutes? 86

6.16 How should minutes be kept? 86

6.17 Does anyone need to sign the minutes? 87

6.18 What use are the minutes? 87

6.19 What can I do if I disagree with the minutes? 87

6.20 Am I entitled to see the minutes? 87

6.21 Who else can see the minutes? 88

Your duties to your co-directors

6.1   Do directors need to hold regular board meetings?

It may be a surprise to you that there is no legal requirement even for large public companies to hold board meetings. Table A is representative of most companies' Articles when it provides that

> "*Subject to the provisions of the articles, the directors may regulate their proceedings as they think fit*".

As directors are usually entrusted with the management of the company, board meetings permit the directors to discuss their company's affairs and to take decisions. Consequently, a certain amount of formality is preferable. Larger companies will establish their own framework for meetings to suit their commercial needs. Even for the smallest company, however, it is a good discipline to establish a framework for holding board meetings. This is particularly so in connection with a director's duty of care (see question 5.2) and in the light of the insolvency legislation (see chapter 15).

The importance of holding board meetings is now supported by the Combined Code. It says that the board should meet regularly. This permits it to retain full and effective control over the company and monitor the executive management. You should, therefore, ensure that your board is supplied with sufficient information to enable it to perform its duties and that it meets sufficiently regularly for you and your fellow directors to manage and administer your company properly.

6.2   How many directors need to attend a board meeting?

Table A provides that the directors may fix the *quorum* of directors necessary to do business at a meeting. A *quorum* is the number of people who must be present at a meeting for it to be validly held. A *quorum is* fixed at two directors, unless the directors decide to change this number. An alternate director counts towards the *quorum* provided that the director who appointed him is not also present at the meeting.

Directors should take care that they maintain a *quorum* at a meeting. The Articles generally provide (see Table A regulation 94) that a director cannot vote on a resolution concerning a matter in which he has a material interest, direct or indirect, that may conflict with the interests of the company. This general prohibition may be relaxed by the Articles and Table A specifies four cases in which it will not apply. Furthermore, he will not count towards the *quorum*. No one knows what precisely is meant by 'material', in this respect, and it is best to err on the side of caution (see question 5.7). If this results in the number of directors present at the meeting, who do not have a material interest in the contract, being less than the *quorum,* the continuing director(s) would have to reconvene the meeting. Alternatively, if the total number of directors having no material interest is less than the quorum, they can act only to appoint additional directors or to call a general meeting of the company. The company in general meeting then has the power to remove the prohibition on the director(s) acting.

6.3   Where should a board meeting be held?

There are no legal restrictions on where a board meeting can be held. This is a matter that is rightly left to the convenience of the directors. Accordingly, there is no reason why a board meeting should not be held outside the country if, for example, a director considers that entering the UK would have adverse personal tax consequences. Technically, a problem might arise because a director absent from the UK is not entitled under Table A to notice of a meeting. However, in practice notice can always be given. In any event, the Articles can be altered should this rule be inconvenient, but you should seek professional advice on how to do this.

A question that often arises in practice is *"can a meeting be held by telephone?"* The answer seems to be that a meeting held by means of a conference call or video conferencing is possible, provided that the Articles contain a carefully worded provision permitting such meetings. All directors should be able to hear and be heard by the others. In addition, the meeting would have to be duly convened. Following the case of *Byng v London Life*

Association [1990] 1 Ch 170 it is thought that the courts will interpret presence at meetings to include presence by means of audio visual links. If you or your fellow directors wish to conduct such a board meeting, professional advice should be sought.

6.4 What notice should be given beforehand?

Table A does not lay down any specific requirement for notice of a meeting to be given. It simply says that any director may call a meeting at any time and the company secretary must do so at his request. This does not mean that no notice at all will suffice. The length of notice given must be reasonable, having regard to the practice of the company and other surrounding circumstances.

It is possible then for an informal and short notice to suffice in the case of a small company where all the directors are in close touch with each other. In contrast, written notice will almost inevitably be necessary in the case of a large company. This is not to say that inadequate notice will suffice in small companies. *Barron v. Potter* [1915] 3 KB 39 was a case involving two directors who met at Paddington Station. One formally proposed the election of three directors and the other objected. The court held that this was not a valid meeting.

Where the notice given for a directors' meeting is unreasonable the meeting will be 'void' in legal terms. This means that it will be treated as if it had never taken place at all. Furthermore, any business conducted at the meeting will also be void. However, one point emerges from both the cases mentioned above – a director who is aggrieved must register his objection at the first possible opportunity.

6.5 Who should be given notice?

Notice should be given to *all* the directors. Otherwise there is a risk that the meeting will be 'void'. The one exception to this provided for in Table A is that notice need not be given to a director who is absent from the UK. There is some doubt in legal circles whether it is necessary for a director who is not entitled to vote at a meeting, for some reason, to be given notice. In practice, it is best to give such a director notice. If it is desired that a director should not even speak at a meeting, the appropriate procedure may be to seek his removal from the board – not to seek his exclusion from meetings.

6.6 What should the notice contain?

In contrast to the notice given of a shareholders' meeting, there are no requirements as to the contents of the notice to be given to directors. In particular, there is no need to state what business is intended to be transacted at the meeting. Clearly, this procedure may be appropriate for small companies, where a degree of flexibility is necessary and the directors are aware of the affairs of the company as a whole. However, it would be highly inappropriate for there to be no indication of the matters to be considered at board meetings of a substantial national or international company. In such companies, for board meetings to serve a useful purpose, there should be circulated, as a minimum, an agenda of proposed business to be transacted. In addition, background papers should be circulated in advance of the meeting, so that informed decisions on important issues affecting the company can be made. These should include regular information as to the company's financial position, for example, by way of management accounts, plans, budgets, etc. This is of particular value where the company has non-executive directors. Unless a non-executive director is well informed he cannot make an effective contribution to the affairs of a company. As noted in question 6.1 above, it is a good discipline for even the smallest company to hold board meetings. Such companies are equally recommended to follow the practice adopted by large companies.

6.7 Should there be a chairman of a board meeting?

Table A permits the directors of a company to appoint a chairman to the board of directors. The chairman must then preside at every board meeting he attends, unless he is unwilling to do so. In that case, or if he is not present at a meeting within five minutes of its commencement, the directors present may elect another chairman for that meeting.

There is, therefore, no legal requirement for there to be a chairman, although practically speaking it is very useful so that meetings are conducted in an efficient manner. A further incentive to appoint a chairman is given in Table A, which provides that where the board cannot reach a decision because there is an equality of votes, the chairman has a second (or 'casting') vote.

The Articles will in general provide that the chairman of the board will preside at general meetings of the company as chairman of those meetings. (See Table A, regulation 42). If the Articles are silent on this point, the members present may elect one of their number to be chairman.

The Cadbury and Hampel Committees saw the role of chairman in a listed company as crucial in securing good corporate governance in that he is primarily responsible for the working of the board and for ensuring that all directors, executive and non-executive alike, are enabled to play their full part in its activities.

6.8   What questions need to be dealt with at a board meeting?

Company law does not provide that directors may transact the company's business only at board meetings. To do so would be impracticable. A company should deal with those questions at board meetings that require the combined experience and skills of the whole board, for example, considering the company's strategy. There is little commercial sense in having valuable board members' time wasted by requiring them to attend a meeting purely, for example, for routine cheque-signing. This is not to say that there is no value in the whole board of a large company exercising a supervisory role over the company's affairs. However, board committees including both executive and non-executive directors are more suited to deal with more routine matters, provided that the committees report regularly to the board.

As discussed above (see question 5.4), in certain circumstances directors must disclose any interest they might have in a company contract to the board, so clearly this is one question that must be dealt with at board meetings.

6.9   What majority is needed for board decisions?

Table A provides that questions arising at any meeting of directors should be decided on a simple majority of votes and that where there is a deadlock, the chairman has a second (or casting vote). Some Articles, however, provide that the chairman has no casting vote. In calculating the majority needed you should bear in mind that in certain circumstances (see question 5.7) some directors may not be entitled to vote. You should also check the Articles of your company to ensure that there is no special provision giving a particular director weighted voting rights.

6.10 Must I attend board meetings?

In legal terms, the need for you to attend board meetings will depend on the circumstances, for example, the number of directors on the board and your own role as a director. As a director, you have a general duty to attend board meetings when you can, but you need not attend all of them. Although it is rare for a director to be sued for negligence, if you failed to attend most board meetings, you could certainly be at risk from such an allegation. Another sanction for non-attendance is provided in Table A, which provides that a director loses his office if he misses meetings for six consecutive months without board permission *and* the directors vote to remove him.

In practical terms, when you accept appointment as a director, you take on certain responsibilities. One of these is the attendance at board meetings. Particularly in a larger company and if you possess a special skill, say, as a Finance Director, then your attendance at board meetings should be an important part of the decision-making process. It also answers the need for a formal cross-fertilisation of ideas within a company, which can be a vital element in the formulation of company strategy.

6.11 Can I be excluded from any board meeting?

No. Ultimately it is the company's shareholders who decide who is to be a director, and it would be wrong if their wishes could be frustrated by a director being excluded from board meeting. A director who is wrongfully excluded in this way can go to court and seek an injunction restraining further exclusion.

6.12 The directors of our company are spread throughout the UK and some abroad. Can we avoid having a formal board meeting?

In some circumstances, you may be able to hold a valid board meeting by telephone (see question 6.3). If you need a resolution to be agreed, Table A provides that a resolution signed by all the directors has the same validity as if it had been passed at a meeting.

6.13 We seem to cover a lot of routine business at board meetings. Can we appoint committees to deal with these matters?

Yes, you can, provided your company's Articles permit it. The general rule is that directors are not able to delegate any of their powers, unless the Articles permit such delegation. However, under Regulation 72 of Table A:

> *"The directors may delegate any of their powers to a committee of one or more directors. They may also delegate to any managing director or any director holding any other executive office such of their powers as they consider desirable to be exercised by him."*

Any such delegation may be subject to conditions and may be revoked at any time by the board. Depending on your company's Articles, your board may have the following options:

- To appoint, as a sub-committee of the board, a committee of directors that can only make recommendations to the board, leaving the board to make the final decisions.

- To appoint a committee or agent to exercise any of the powers of the board without further reference to it. (This option should be considered in the light of the recommendation of the Combined Code that the board should have a formal schedule of matters specifically reserved to it for decision (see question 4.1 above).

The Combined Code, in fact, recommends that, generally, the boards of listed companies should set up a nomination committee (to make recommendations to the board on any new appointments to it), an audit committee (as a minimum to review the company's annual and half-yearly financial statements before submission to the board and liaising with the auditors), and a remuneration committee (to recommend to the board the remuneration of executive directors).

6.14 Do minutes of board meetings need to be taken?

Yes. The Companies Act 1985 requires every company to cause minutes to be kept of all directors' meetings and meetings of managers. Furthermore, Table A requires the directors to cause minutes to be kept of the appointment of all officers made by the directors and of the proceedings at all directors' meetings including the names of the directors present.

6.15 What should be recorded in the minutes?

Although Table A refers to a record of 'proceedings', no one would expect the minutes to record details of the discussions at a meeting. Rather, they are a record of the actual decisions taken. However, in some instances directors may wish to record the reasons for their decisions. The writing of good minutes of meetings is an art. It requires conciseness, accuracy, objectivity and the absence of any ambiguity.

6.16 How should minutes be kept?

Responsibility for the keeping of minutes usually falls on the company secretary (see question 2.20). In practice, any person attending a meeting can be asked to take the minutes of it and an ordinary secretary can be invited to attend for this purpose. The minutes must be entered in 'books kept for the purpose'. Under the 1985 Act minutes should be kept either by making entries in a bound book or by recording them by some other means, which is adequate to avoid falsification.

There is no requirement that the minute books must be kept in any particular place nor that anyone can inspect them. If the minutes are not properly kept both the company and every officer of it will be liable to a fine of £1,000, and, for continued contravention, to a daily default fine of £100.

6.17 Does anyone need to sign the minutes?

No. Although the Companies Act 1985 provides that a minute signed by the chairman of a meeting or the next succeeding meeting is evidence of the proceedings at that meeting, there is no legal requirement that anyone should sign them.

Contrary to common belief, there is no need for the board to confirm or adopt the minutes of a previous meeting, although it is doubtlessly good practice. If the directors approve the minutes of a meeting in some way it will be difficult subsequently for a director to deny his collective responsibility for any decision.

6.18 What use are the minutes?

As noted above, minutes signed by the chairman are evidence of the proceedings at a meeting. The Companies Act 1985 does not, however, deem them to be conclusive evidence of what has happened at a meeting, although there is nothing to prevent the company's Articles from containing such a provision. Therefore, if a matter to which the minutes relate should ever come before a court, it is possible to submit alternative evidence to show that the minutes are incomplete or inaccurate.

6.19 What can I do if I disagree with the minutes?

You should state your objection at the first possible opportunity. However, you are at the mercy of the chairman (if he takes responsibility for the minutes) as to whether or not your objection is formally recorded. If that happens, you would be wise to consider some other documentary means of recording your objection, and, depending on the seriousness of the matter, you may also need to seek professional advice.

6.20 Am I entitled to see the minutes?

There is no statutory right that entitles you to see them, nor any right in Table A. However, the courts recognise the need for a director to be able to see minutes of board meetings as he may be called to account for matters included in them. Consequently, at common law you have the right to see the minutes.

6.21 Who else can see the minutes?

The auditors of your company have a statutory right of access to the company's books and this includes board minutes. However, a company's shareholders and other persons do not have that right.

Chapter 7

Your accounting and financial responsibilities

Question *Page*

7.1   Why do companies have to produce financial statements? 91

7.2   As a director, do I have any responsibility for the financial statements? 92

7.3   My company does not need an audit. What statement should I make? 93

7.4   Do I have any other duties in connection with the financial statements? 93

7.5   Is compliance with these requirements all that is necessary? 94

7.6   What accounting records must a company keep? 94

7.7   How long must accounting records be kept? 97

7.8   Where can my company keep its accounting records? 98

7.9   Can my company keep its accounting records outside Great Britain? 98

7.10   Am I entitled to see my company's accounting records? 98

7.11   Can anyone else see my company's accounting records? 98

7.12   What if proper accounting records are not kept? 99

7.13   My company has taken the exemption not to have its financial statements audited. Does this make any difference? 100

7.14   What accounts must be prepared? 100

7.15 Can I leave all the responsibility for the financial statements
with the finance director? 101

7.16 Should my company have internal auditors? 101

7.17 Should my company have an audit committee? 102

7.18 Do the financial statements have to be prepared by a
certain date? 103

7.19 What happens if my company is late in filing its financial
statements 103

7.20 What other penalties are there for non-compliance? 104

7.21 What formalities are there for paying a dividend? 104

7.22 Are there any restrictions on the size of dividends my company
can pay? 105
       Private companies 105
       Public companies 106

7.23 What happens if a dividend is excessive? 106

7.24 I'm a director of a small company. I have heard about the
year 2000 problem. Should I be worried? 106
       Are there any other problems? 107

Your accounting and financial responsibilities

7.1 Why do companies have to produce financial statements?

Companies have had to produce financial statements (referred to under the Companies Act as 'accounts') and to circulate them to members since the beginning of the century. The purpose of making financial information available in the form of the company's annual financial statements is primarily to provide an account of the stewardship of the directors during that year to assist shareholders and debenture holders in the informed exercise of their rights. So far as shareholders are concerned, this is interpreted as meaning *"to enable them to question the past management of the company, to exercise voting rights, if so advised, and to influence future policy and management"*. [*Caparo Industries plc v. Dickman* [1990] BCC per Lord Jauncey of Tullichettle at p.203]. The financial statements that have to be prepared are required to give 'a true and fair view' of the company's financial position and profit or loss. Great care is, therefore, required in their preparation and deliberate overstatement or understatement conflicts with this requirement.

The Companies Act 1985 as amended by the Companies Act 1989 contains the statutory rules that have to be observed in the preparation of financial statements. In addition, the Accounting Standards Board (ASB) publishes rules for accountants known as Financial Reporting Standards (FRSs). The ASB replaced the Accounting Standards Committee which previously issued Statements of Standard Accounting Practice (SSAPs). FRSs and SSAPs set out methods of accounting and disclosure to be adopted in respect of all financial statements intended to give a true and fair view. Under ASB, accounting standards now have a degree of legal backing and need to be observed. Financial statements must now state whether they have been prepared in accordance with applicable accounting standards and particulars of and reasons for any material departure have to be given.

7.2   As a director, do I have any responsibility for the financial statements?

Yes. This is the case even though the rules regarding the preparation of financial statements are very complex; in fact, unless you are an accountant it is unlikely that you will be fully aware of all of them. Nevertheless, it is the directors' responsibility to prepare financial statements for each financial year, consisting of a balance sheet and a profit and loss account and related notes, which comply with the requirements of the Companies Act 1985. You will, therefore, need to gain an understanding of how the financial statements have been prepared. A statement acknowledging directors' responsibility for keeping accounting records and preparing financial statements is now required to be included in a company's annual report, whether audited or unaudited.

Statement to be made where financial statements are audited

The Cadbury Committee recommended that a brief statement of directors' responsibilities for the financial statements should appear in the annual report of UK listed companies immediately before the auditors' report (which includes a statement of the auditors' responsibilities). Appendix 3 of the Cadbury Report provides guidance on the matters that would need to be covered by the directors' statement. The purpose of this statement is to make it clear that responsibility for preparing the financial statements rests with the board of directors and to remove any misconception that the auditors are responsible for the financial statements. This recommendation has been included in the best practice provisions of the Combined Code.

If your company's financial statements do not give an adequate description of the directors' responsibilities for the financial statements, your company's auditors are required to do so in their auditors' report.

In addition, auditors are required to distinguish between their responsibilities and those of the directors by including in their auditors' report: a statement that the financial statements are the responsibility of the directors; a reference to the statement of responsibilities made by the directors (and, if there is no reference to include one); and a statement that the auditors' responsibility is to express an opinion on the financial statements.

7.3 My company does not need an audit. What statement should I make?

A statement of responsibilities must be made by you and your fellow directors even if your company qualifies for the audit exemption under section 249A of the 1985 Act (see question 2.23). For your company to be entitled to the exemption from audit, the statement must acknowledge your responsibilities for:

- Ensuring that the company keeps accounting records that comply with section 221 of the 1985 Act (see question 7.6).

- Preparing financial statements that give a true and fair view of the state of affairs of the company as at the end of the financial year and of its profit and loss for the financial year in accordance with the requirements of section 226 of the 1985 Act, and which otherwise comply with the requirements of the Act relating to financial statements, so far as applicable to the company.

The statement must appear in the balance sheet above the signature of the director who signs on behalf of the board.

7.4 Do I have any other duties in connection with the financial statements?

As a director you also have a duty:

- To ensure that accounting records sufficient to show and explain your company's transactions are kept. This is explained in more detail below.

- In addition to preparing them, to approve annual financial statements that comply with the requirements of the Companies Act 1985.

- To ensure that the company sends copies of the annual financial statements, including the directors' report and the auditors' report to every shareholder and other person entitled to receive them.

- To lay the annual financial statements including the directors' report and the auditors' report before shareholders in general meeting (unless your company, as a private company, has validly elected to dispense with the laying of financial statements).

- To deliver the financial statements including the directors' report and the auditors' report to the Registrar within the period permitted by the Companies Act 1985.

7.5 Is compliance with these requirements all that is necessary?

The statutory rules are generally considered to set out the minimum requirements with regard to a company's accounting records. Established or larger businesses are likely to have sophisticated computerised systems that will provide statistical and management information as well as the financial information that is required for the preparation of the annual financial statements. However, whatever types of accounting system your company has, they must be sufficient to provide you with such regular information as is necessary for you to discharge your duties as a director. Internal controls should, therefore, be established by management in order to carry on the company's business in an orderly and efficient manner, to ensure adherence to management policies and safeguard the assets, as well as to secure as far as possible the completeness and accuracy of the records. The exact measures taken by a company will depend on its size and complexity amongst other things.

7.6 What accounting records must a company keep?

All companies are under a duty to keep accounting records. This is required by section 221 of the 1985 Act. The accounting records must be sufficient to *"show and explain the company's transactions"*. Furthermore, they must disclose the financial position of the company with reasonable accuracy *at any time* and enable the company's directors to ensure that its statutory financial statements comply with the Companies Act 1985 in terms of their form and content. An unorganised collection of vouchers and documents is not sufficient; the accounting records must enable a trial balance to be constructed from them. This means that the records must be updated consistently throughout the year and not just when the statutory financial statements are being prepared. The 1985 Acts says that accounting records should in particular contain:

■ Daily entries of receipts and payments with details of what they are for.

■ A record of the company's assets and liabilities.

■ Where the company deals in goods, year-end stock records and any records from which these are prepared.

■ Where the company deals in goods, records of all goods bought and sold, with enough detail to identify the buyers and sellers. No such record needs to be kept in the case of retail goods.

This is not the end of the story, however, and when considering the requirements governing a company's accounting records you must take into account other requirements, particularly the tax and VAT legislation, which are outside the scope of this book.

The Institute of Chartered Accountants in England and Wales has published a booklet entitled 'Financial and accounting responsibilities of directors', originally issued as a Technical Release (TECH 28/96), in November 1996 to provide guidance for directors on their main financial and accounting duties and responsibilities. As best practice it recommends that:

> *"In addition to the statutory requirement to keep proper accounting records, the directors have an overriding responsibility to ensure that they have adequate information to enable them to discharge their duty to manage the company's business.*
>
> *The duty to manage the company's business will involve ensuring that adequate control is kept over its records and transactions, for example:*
>
> *(a) cash;*
> *(b) debtors and creditors;*
> *(c) stock and work in progress;*

(d) capital expenditure; and
(e) major contracts.

The nature and extent of the accounting and management information needed to exercise this control will depend upon the nature and extent of the company's business.

To restrict the possibility of actions for wrongful trading, directors will constantly need to be aware of the company's financial position and progress, and the accounting records should be sufficient to enable them to be provided with the information required for drawing conclusions on these matters. The directors should also be satisfied that proper systems to provide them with regular and prompt information are in place.

Directors must also be aware of a company's prospects. It may therefore be prudent to prepare a plan against which the subsequent performance of the business can be measured. Periodic management accounts assist in enabling the actual operating results and cash position to be compared with the plan. Once again, the need for, extent and frequency of the preparation of such accounts and the level of management to which they are presented will depend upon the size, scope and nature of the business. However, the directors' report on the financial statements must contain an indication of the likely future developments in the business of the company and its subsidiary undertakings (Companies Act 1985, Schedule 7), and a plan is likely to be helpful in this context."

In practice, a company's accounting records would include records of:

- Cash.
- Sales.
- Sales returns.
- Purchases.
- Purchase returns.
- Creditors.
- Debtors.

■   Other assets, liabilities and expenses.

Company law permits these to be retained on a computer (although bear in mind Customs & Excise and tax requirements referred to above), or in other suitable readable form. These accounting records form the basis of what is called a 'double-entry bookkeeping system'. If you are incorporating an existing business you may already be familiar with such a system. If you are setting up in business for the first time, your accountants will be able to help you decide on a system appropriate for your business and help to explain how it can be operated.

Your record-keeping obligations do not finish with your accounting records, although these are very important. There are various payroll records that you must keep, for example, as to statutory sick pay (see appendix II paragraph (vii)). Depending on the type of information you store and the way in which you store it, you may need to comply with the laws relating to the protection of personal data currently contained in the Data Protection Act 1984 – in due course to be replaced by the Data Protection Act 1998. Specialised types of business may also be subject to special requirements. For example, if you are an 'investment business' you will have to comply with various record-keeping requirements so as to comply with the Financial Services Act 1986.

7.7   How long must accounting records be kept?

Company law only requires a private company to keep its accounting records for three years from the date when they are prepared and a public company for six years. However, there are a number of other considerations. For example, all companies registered for VAT must keep certain records for at least six years. A similar minimum period is recommended for records related to tax generally, since the Inland Revenue can normally assess you for tax at any time up to six years after a chargeable period. For VAT purposes you will need to keep the necessary records for six years, and as an employer, your company should keep the relevant documents relating to PAYE for at least three years However, you should consult your legal advisers for any specific rules applicable to your business.

In commercial terms, the view is frequently taken that all records should be destroyed as soon as possible to save storage space and therefore cost. However, modern methods of scanning and microfilming enable documents to be retained at little cost in legible form. If you are setting up in business for the first time you should discuss the period necessary for keeping your particular records with your professional advisors. If your company is established and substantial, you should consider nominating a person to be responsible for document retention so that a consistent policy is applied and maintained.

7.8 Where can my company keep its accounting records?

A company can keep its accounting records either at its registered office or any other place that the directors decide upon.

7.9 Can my company keep its accounting records outside Great Britain?

Yes. However, if the company does so, 'accounts and returns' must be sent to an appropriate place in Great Britain (for example, the company's registered office) where they must be available for inspection at all times by the company's officers. These accounts and returns should show the company's financial position at intervals not exceeding six months. They should also enable the directors to ensure that the company's financial statements comply with the rules on form and content set out in the Companies Act 1985 (see question 7.6).

7.10 Am I entitled to see my company's accounting records?

Yes. Although the accounting records are usually made the responsibility of one particular director (for example, the Finance Director) they must be available for inspection by the company's officers at all times. A company's officers include its directors and the company secretary.

7.11 Can anyone else see my company's accounting records?

Your auditors also have a statutory right of access to your company's books, accounts and vouchers; and they are entitled to require you to give such information and explanations as they think necessary for the performance of their duties as auditors.

7.12 What if proper accounting records are not kept?

First, where a company fails to keep or preserve accounting records *every* officer of the company who is in default commits a criminal offence under the Companies Act 1985, *unless* he can show that he acted honestly and that the default was excusable in the circumstances in which the company's business was carried on. However, an offence will be committed where an officer of a company fails to take all reasonable steps to ensure that the company keeps these accounting records for the required period, *or* has intentionally caused any default by the company in this respect. If a person is convicted on trial on indictment he can be imprisoned for a maximum of two years and/or given an unlimited fine. On summary trial he can be imprisoned for a maximum of six months and/or given a fine of up to £5,000. A table of criminal offences is given in appendix V.

You should remember that your company's auditors are placed under a specific duty to carry out such investigations as will enable them to form an opinion as to whether your company has kept proper accounting records and whether proper returns adequate for their audit have been received from branches not visited by them. If they cannot come to such an opinion, or their opinion has to be qualified in some way, this will be mentioned in their audit report. Although that may not sound a serious sanction, remember that it may come to the attention of the DTI, Customs & Excise and the Inland Revenue, or possibly concern your company's bankers. The consequences could then be serious.

In summary, if you and your fellow directors do not ensure that proper accounting records are kept, you are unlikely to have sufficient up-to-date financial information to manage the company's business properly. In addition, you should remember that the extent of your responsibility for a failure by your company to comply with the company law provision in respect of company records could have further implications. Failure to keep accounting records is a factor that could later be taken into account by a court assessing whether a director is 'unfit' to be a director and should, therefore, be disqualified (see question 13.3).

7.13 My company has taken the exemption not to have its financial statements audited. Does this make any difference?

Even if your company has taken the exemption available to certain small companies not to have its financial statements audited it is important for you to ensure that the company keeps proper accounting records. You may still be liable under the 1985 Act if your company does not keep proper accounting records and, therefore, risk being assessed by a court to be 'unfit' to be a director.

7.14 What accounts must be prepared?

The directors of every company are responsible for the company preparing:

- A profit and loss account (or an income and expenditure account if the company does not trade for profit), in respect of each financial year of the company.

- A balance sheet as at the last date of the company's financial year.

- A directors' report, for each financial year.

- Consolidated financial statements, where a company has subsidiary undertakings at its year end (unless the group it heads qualifies as a small group and does not include a bank, insurance company or a company authorised under the Financial Services Act 1986).

In addition, accounting standards require companies to prepare a cash flow statement and a statement of total recognised gains and losses. This book uses the term 'financial statements', which is a term adopted by the accounting bodies to refer to the accounts, that is, the profit and loss account, balance sheet, cash flow statement and statement of total recognised gains and losses. Many listed companies also include an operating and financial review in their annual report.

All companies must prepare their financial statements on the basis of standard formats set out in the Companies Act 1985. These standard formats are in use throughout the European Community. In addition, there are detailed requirements for the content of company financial statements. The key legal requirement, however, is that the profit and loss account and balance sheet must give 'a true and fair view' of the company's or group's profit or loss for the financial year and its state of affairs at the end of that year. You can find detailed information about the legal and accounting requirements in PricewaterhouseCoopers' Manual of Accounting published by Gee.

7.15 Can I leave all the responsibility for the financial statements with the finance director?

No. As you have seen, company law places the duty to prepare a company's financial statements on the directors of a company. Although much of the detailed work relating to this will (and ought to) be undertaken by the Finance Director this does not absolve other directors from their overall responsibility. Even where your company has an audit committee, the ultimate responsibility for reviewing and approving the report and financial statements remains with the board. As considered below (see question 13.5), the way in which you discharge this responsibility could affect a decision as to whether you are disqualified as a director.

The directors' collective responsibility for the financial statements is also indicated by the legal requirement that the financial statements must be approved by the board and then one of the directors of the company must sign its balance sheet (and the copy filed with the Registrar) *on behalf of* the board.

7.16 Should my company have internal auditors?

It has been mentioned earlier that the directors' duty to manage the company's business involves ensuring that adequate control is kept over its records and transactions. Larger companies have increasingly created an internal audit department as an aid to control. An internal audit function can significantly improve internal control, by monitoring internal accounting controls, by reviewing budgetary control and management systems, or by carrying out operational audits in key risk areas (for instance in manufacturing businesses the main priority may be operational efficiency).

Cadbury considered it good practice to set up an internal audit function to undertake regular monitoring of key controls and procedures (but did not include this in the Cadbury Code). The Hampel Committee supported this and, although it saw no need for a hard and fast rule, it suggested that companies should review from time to time the need for a separate internal audit function. This was on the basis that the work of the external auditors will not necessarily cover the full scope of the controls.

7.17 Should my company have an audit committee?

There are no statutory requirements concerning audit committees but, particularly in larger companies, such committees provide a useful mechanism for regular contact between the company's auditors and the board. Many audit committees will confine themselves to those duties most closely related to the financial statements, for example to review the draft annual report prior to their approval by the board. It is generally thought that contact between the external auditors and directors outside the finance function is good and assists in promoting objectivity and independence in the preparation and audit of the financial statements.

The Combined Code recommends that boards should establish audit committees, with written terms of reference, made up of at least three non-executive directors. The majority of these directors should be independent and they should be named in the annual report. Most larger listed companies have set up audit committees.

In addition, the Audit Faculty of the Institute of Chartered Accountants in England and Wales produced in May 1997 a booklet entitled *Audit Committees – A Framework for Assessment*. This develops guidance already given in a previous booklet to incorporate some of the good practices that are emerging in connection with audit committees. Although the booklet says that it is based primarily on experience of audit committees in the plc sector, it states that many of the questions and ideas are equally relevant in the context of smaller entities, not-for-profit organisations and the public sector.

7.18 Do the financial statements have to be prepared by a certain date?

Yes, the directors must ensure that they comply with the statutory timescale for laying the company's financial statements for each financial year before the shareholders and delivering them to the Registrar. For a private company, the period for laying and delivering financial statements is ten months (seven months for a public company) after the end of the company's accounting reference period. (Listed companies are required to publish their financial statements as soon as possible after they have been approved and in any event within six months of the end of the financial period to which they relate.)

A company's accounting reference periods are determined according to its accounting reference date. Each company must have an accounting reference date and, for companies incorporated after 1 April 1990, it is the last day of the month in which the anniversary of incorporation falls. A company's first accounting reference period is the period of more than six months, but not more than 18 months, beginning with the date of its incorporation and ending on its accounting reference date. Each subsequent accounting reference period will be for 12 months, starting immediately after the end of the previous accounting reference period.

A company may, in certain circumstances, alter its accounting reference date by sending Form 225 to the Registrar of companies before the end of the period allowed for filing the financial statements in question.

7.19 What happens if my company is late in filing its financial statements?

The Registrar has power to impose a fine on a company if its annual accounts and the directors' report and auditors' report (its financial statements) are not delivered to the Registrar within the period allowed. This period is mentioned in the paragraphs above. The fine will depend on the lateness in filing. For instance, a private company that files not more than three months late will incur a fine of £100, from three to six months late the fine is £250, from six to twelve months it is £500 and over twelve months, £1,000. Public companies incur fines which are four to five times larger.

Under the Company Directors Disqualification Act 1986 a director who is persistently in default in filing any return, account or other document to be filed with or delivered to the Registrar, may be disqualified if he has had three or more default orders, for instance, under sections 242 or 245B, made against him in the five years ending with the date of the application.

7.20 What other penalties are there for non-compliance?

Additionally, company law prescribes penalties where financial statements or consolidated financial statements that do not comply with the requirements of the Companies Act 1985 are approved by the directors. On trial on indictment *all* the directors are liable to an unlimited fine, or on summary trial a fine to a maximum of £5,000. It is a defence, however, if you can show that you took all reasonable steps to prevent their being approved.

The Companies Act 1985 allows for the voluntary revision by the directors of the financial statements or directors' report where it appears that the financial statements or report did not comply with the requirements of the 1985 Act. It also permits the Secretary of State to require the revision of defective financial statements. In practice, public and large private companies are dealt with by the Financial Reporting Review Panel; the Department of Trade and Industry deals with other companies.

7.21 What formalities are there for paying a dividend?

These are set out in a company's Articles of association. Usually the Articles will provide that the company may by ordinary resolution declare dividends, but that no dividend shall exceed the amount recommended by the directors. The directors may also have the power to pay interim dividends. (See Regulations 102 and 103 of Table A.) The Articles generally only set out the procedure to be followed by the directors regarding dividends, but they sometimes contain certain restrictions. A company may also be subject to restrictions under contract, for instance, a loan agreement.

7.22 Are there any restrictions on the size of dividends my company can pay?

Yes. The basic rule restricting the size of dividends is that they must only be paid out of profits which are available for the purpose. The extent of the restrictions, however, will depend upon whether your company is a private company or a public company. The rules for establishing what profits are available are complex and, therefore, the following is only intended as a general guide.

Private companies

A company's profits available for distribution are, basically, its accumulated, realised profits less its accumulated, realised losses. The principles are summarised below:

- Realised profits and realised losses must be 'accumulated' from one year to the next. So if you make a loss in one year, this must be made good by profits accumulated in subsequent (and/or previous) years before a distribution can be made.

- Only 'realised' profits can be distributed. Whether a profit is 'realised' or 'unrealised' has to be determined in accordance with generally accepted accounting principles. For example, in general, a revaluation of an asset does not give rise to a 'realised' profit.

- In calculating your accumulated realised profit or loss you must take into account any distributions or capitalisation already made and any losses written off in a capital reduction or reorganisation.

The amount of the intended dividend must be justified by reference to the company's profits as shown in its 'relevant accounts', usually the company's last annual financial statements. If the last annual financial statements do not show sufficient available profits, the directors will need to prepare financial statements (known as interim accounts) which enable a reasonable judgment to be made as to whether the company has sufficient profits to justify the dividend.

However, even if the relevant accounts show sufficient profits to cover the proposed dividend, you should take account of your common law duties. The directors have a duty to act in the company's best interests generally. A dividend paid, for instance, without regard to the company's future cash needs (for example, where they know it will be incurring losses) or imprudently, may be a breach of this duty. In addition, the common law rule is that a distribution cannot be made out of capital. The directors, therefore, would need to consider whether the company's profits as shown in the relevant accounts have since been wiped out by subsequent losses before paying a dividend based on those accounts.

Public companies

The principles that apply to private companies apply equally to public companies, but there are additional, and more stringent, requirements; Principally, accumulated unrealised losses must be made good. In addition, if a public company needs to prepare interim accounts (because the last annual financial statements do not show sufficient profits), those financial statements must be properly prepared and comply with section 226 and Schedule 4 of the 1985 Act and must be filed with the Registrar before payment of the dividend.

There are further special provisions that relate to investment and insurance companies.

7.23 What happens if a dividend is excessive?

A shareholder is liable to repay a dividend to his company if he knew, or had reasonable grounds to believe, that it exceeded the profits available for distribution. Furthermore, the directors may be held liable to the company if it appears that they had paid a dividend without having sufficient realised reserves to do so.

7.24 I'm a director of a small company. I have heard about the year 2000 problem. Should I be worried?

Probably. The problem affects mainframe and personal computers and any device containing a microprocessor chip that manipulates dates. This includes telephones, answering machines, fax machines, photocopiers, lifts, air conditioning, lighting, clocks, timers and fire and burglar alarms. If, therefore, your company has a computerised system for keeping or processing accounting records or a computer system which is essential to the continued trading of the company, you are likely to need to set up your own year 2000 programme to ensure such key systems are 'year 2000 compliant' by 31 December 1999. Most businesses (small and large alike) will, therefore, be affected.

If you have not already done so you should consider obtaining advice from a computer consultant to identity the steps needed to ensure your systems will be able to recognise that 1 January 2000 follows 31 December 1999. This could extend to studying your existing contracts for computer services or software to see who is responsible for dealing with problems. The older your computer system the more likely it is that the supplier will be able to argue that there was no implied warranty that the system would be year 2000 compliant. You should also ensure that any new computer equipment or software you acquire is compliant. It may be necessary for you to take legal advice. These points, however, are only indicative of some of the matters you should be considering. The earlier you act to identify and resolve the potential problems the more chance you have of beating the deadline!

Are there any other problems?

Yes. The year 2000 problem is not limited to a company's own systems. If your suppliers are not 'year 2000 compliant' your company's business could also be affected even though your systems are. For instance, if your suppliers are not able to fulfil their contractual obligations to your company because they are not year 2000 compliant, you may, in turn, be unable to meet your own contractual obligations to your customers. You may, therefore, need to consider what action to take if there is doubt whether your suppliers' systems will permit them to meet their commitments to you on and after 1 January 2000.

Chapter 8

Shareholders' meetings

Question   *Page*

8.1   What is a shareholders' meeting? 111

8.2   Does the company need to hold regular meetings? 111

8.3   What has to be done at an annual general meeting? 111

8.4   Who is responsible for arranging the annual general meeting? . . 113

8.5   When must an extraordinary general meeting be held? 113

8.6   How much notice should be given for a shareholders' meeting? . 114

8.7   What is special notice? 114

8.8   Where should a shareholders' meeting be held? 115

8.9   Do all the directors have to be present at a shareholders'
        meeting? 116

8.10 Should there be a chairman of a shareholders' meeting? 116

8.11 Can I attend a shareholders' meeting if I am not a shareholder? . 116

8.12 How many shareholders need to attend a shareholders'
        meeting? 117

8.13 What majority is needed for a resolution to be passed at a
        shareholders' meeting? 118

8.14 I have heard of elective resolutions – what are they? 120

8.15 What is the written resolution procedure? 120

8.16 What happens after a resolution is adopted at a general
meeting? 121

Shareholders' meetings

8.1   What is a shareholders' meeting?

As noted earlier, the shareholders of a company are its owners. As a director you are responsible for the company's management and, therefore, accountable to the company's owners. At a shareholders' meeting the shareholders meet formally and may discuss and determine the company's future, taking the decisions that are, by law or by the company's Articles, required of them.

8.2   Does the company need to hold regular meetings?

There must be an 'annual general meeting' ('AGM') which must be held in each calendar year and within 15 months of the last such meeting, unless the company has elected to dispense with the holding of one (see question 8.14). Where a company is newly incorporated the first AGM must be held within 18 months of incorporation. It would be unusual for a company to have any other regular meeting, but this is possible. Any other meeting is called an 'extraordinary general meeting' ('EGM'). This type of meeting is considered in question 8.5 below.

8.3   What has to be done at an annual general meeting?

This will depend on the company's Articles.

Table A requires only that the retirement of a company's first directors is considered at the first AGM and that the retirement of directors by rotation is considered at each AGM.

In practice, it is also customary (and convenient) for an annual general meeting to cover the following:

- The adoption of the financial statements for the most recent financial year.
- Reading the audit report on the financial statements to the meeting.
- The declaration of any dividend payable.
- The election or re-election of the directors.
- A resolution to (re)appoint the auditors and to pay them a fee or empower the directors to fix the amount.

Some companies will have adopted Table A prior to 1 July 1985 when the new Table A was introduced. (The earlier Table A is referred to as 'the old Table A'.) The changes in the new Table A do not apply to companies in existence at that date, unless specifically adopted by them. Under the new Table A an indication of all business must be given in the notice of the meeting. In the case of an AGM the notice must specify the meeting to be such.

If your company is subject to the old Table A, you will find that its Articles distinguish between 'ordinary' business and 'special' business. 'Special' business can only be validly transacted if its general nature is summarised in the notice to the meeting. 'Ordinary' business under the old Table A consisted of the declaration of a dividend, consideration of the accounts, balance sheets and directors' and auditors' reports, the election of directors in place of those retiring, and the appointment of auditors and the fixing of their remuneration. 'Special' business was anything else.

Your company's register of directors' interests in shares and debentures must be produced at the commencement of the AGM and remain open and accessible during the meeting to any person attending it (see question 11.8).

If the company in question is listed on the Stock Exchange, the Stock Exchange's Listing Rules additionally requires that copies of all directors' service contracts of more than one year's duration or, where a contract is not in writing, a memorandum of its terms, must be made available for inspection by any person at the company's registered office on each business day during usual business hours. They must also be made available at the place of the annual general meeting for at least 15 minutes prior to the meeting and at the meeting itself.

8.4 Who is responsible for arranging the annual general meeting?

In practice, the company secretary will be delegated the responsibility of arranging the AGM. However, legally both the company and all its officers are responsible for any failure to hold an AGM. The maximum penalty on trial on indictment is an unlimited fine. On summary trial the penalty is limited to a fine of £5,000.

8.5 When must an extraordinary general meeting be held?

Table A leaves it to you, as the directors of a company, to call an EGM whenever you think fit. You must, however, call an EGM in the following situations:

- *Shareholders 'requisition'*
  The directors have to call an EGM where shareholders holding at least ten per cent of the paid up voting share capital of the company formally require this. The formal 'requisition' must state the purpose of the meeting, be signed by those requiring the meeting and be deposited at the company's registered office. If the directors do not call the meeting within 21 days to be held no later than 28 days thereafter, then those who requisitioned the meeting (or holders of more than half their voting rights) may call the meeting themselves within three months. The company will then have to pay the expenses of this meeting and must deduct it from the directors' remuneration.

- *Court order*
  Where for any reason it is impracticable for a meeting to be called or conducted in the way prescribed by a company's Articles or by law, a court may order an EGM to be called, held and conducted in any manner it thinks fit. It may also do so on the application of a director or member entitled to vote at the meeting.

- *Serious loss of the company's capital*
  The directors of a public company must call an EGM if their company suffers a serious loss of capital, where its net assets fall to half or less of its called up share capital. The meeting must be called no later than 28 days from the earliest day on which the loss is known to a director

of the company and must actually be held at a date no later than 56 days from that date. The purpose of the meeting is to consider whether (and if so, what) steps should be taken to deal with the situation. If no meeting is called, each director who 'knowingly and wilfully' authorises the failure to call the meeting (or subsequently permits the failure to continue) is liable on conviction on indictment to an unlimited fine, or on summary trial to a fine up to a maximum of £5,000.

In addition, the Articles may permit shareholders to call a meeting themselves – see regulation 37 of Table A.

8.6 How much notice should be given for a shareholders' meeting?

The law requires 21 days' written notice to be given for an AGM, unless the shareholders entitled to vote *all* agree to a shorter period. For other meetings 14 days' notice must be given unless the holders of 95 per cent of the share capital with voting rights agree to a shorter period. A company's Articles *may* specify longer periods than these, but this is unusual.

The courts have taken the view that 'days' mean 'clear days', and so you should exclude the day that a shareholder receives the notice and the day of the meeting itself in counting the number of days. For example, if you wish to hold an annual general meeting on 27 March, you must ensure that the notice is posted no later than 3 March. The reason for the additional two days is that Table A states that a notice will be deemed to be given at the expiration of 48 hours after the envelope containing it was posted. You are well advised in any event to leave ample time for the notice to be received and also to retain proof that the envelopes containing the notice were properly addressed, prepaid and posted. This is because Table A deems that such proof is *conclusive* evidence that you have given the notice.

8.7 What is special notice?

There are certain types of resolution for which 'special notice' must be given to the company. Special notice is notice to the company of the intention by one or more members to put forward a particular resolution at a meeting. It must be given no less than 28 days before the meeting. However, even if a meeting is subsequently called in less than the required period, the notice is deemed to have been validly given. Otherwise the directors could frustrate the purpose of a resolution (for example, to remove a director) by calling a meeting at short notice and then arguing that any dismissal was invalid.

When the company receives a special notice it must give notice of the intended resolution to its shareholders at the same time and in the same way as it gives notice of the meeting. If that is impracticable, it must advertise the notice in a newspaper of 'appropriate circulation' (or as otherwise permitted in the company's Articles) no less than 21 days before the meeting.

The circumstances where special notice of a resolution is required include:

■ To appoint or retain a director of a public company, or of its subsidiary, who has reached 70 years of age.

■ Where the effect of certain resolutions is to appoint a new auditor or to remove an old auditor before the expiration of his term of office.

■ To remove a director before the term for which he was appointed has expired.

8.8 Where should a shareholders' meeting be held?

There are no legal restrictions on where a shareholders' meeting should be held. This will be a practical question for the directors to consider. In a small private company where the directors are the only shareholders, the directors may decide to hold their meeting either at the company's place of business, or at their homes, or in the board room that many firms of accountants make available for this purpose. The possibility of holding a meeting by telephone is considered, in the context of board meetings, in question 6.3. One difference in relation to shareholders' meetings is that, unless the Articles provide otherwise, the *quorum* for a meeting can only be constituted by shareholders attending *personally*. Although Table A makes provision for attendance by proxy or by an authorised representative of a company, there is no provision for the meeting to be held other than in person. See, however, the written resolution procedure described in question 8.15.

8.9 Do all the directors have to be present at a shareholders' meeting?

No. In fact Table A specifically caters for the situation where there is no director present at all, in that it permits the shareholders to elect one of themselves to chair the meeting if no director arrives within 15 minutes of the time for which the meeting is called.

At a company's AGM, particularly in the case of a large company, it is advisable for all directors to attend. Often the AGM is the only occasion when the directors of a company can be called to account for their stewardship of the company and answer questions. Frequently, a question can only be meaningfully and accurately answered by the director responsible for the particular area of the company's business. However, there may be an EGM held for a particular purpose where your attendance may be unnecessary.

8.10 Should there be a chairman of a shareholders' meeting?

Yes. If the directors have elected a chairman of the board of directors (see question 6.7), Table A provides that he should preside as chairman of a shareholders' meeting. Where the chairman of the board is neither present, nor willing to act, within 15 minutes of the meeting commencing, the directors present must elect one of themselves as chairman. If only one director is present, he must act as chairman if he is willing to do so. Failing this, Table A provides that the shareholders present who can vote must choose one of themselves to be chairman of the meeting.

8.11 Can I attend a shareholders' meeting if I am not a shareholder?

You are entitled as a director under Table A to attend and speak at any shareholders' meeting whether or not you are a shareholder.

Those who are neither shareholders, nor directors, are not entitled to attend, although some public companies will permit outsiders to attend, for example, members of the Press.

8.12 How many shareholders need to attend a shareholders' meeting?

Unless your company's Articles provide otherwise, the Companies Act 1985 states that there must be two shareholders present in person to constitute a meeting. The new Table A varies this by providing that personal attendance can include attendance by proxy or by an authorised representative of a company.

However, in the case of a private company which has a single member, this rule is modified to enable one member present in person or by proxy to be a quorum, notwithstanding anything in the company's Articles.

You should note that if a shareholder dies his personal representative will become entitled to his shareholding. Frequently, a personal representative will not actually give notice to the company requesting to be entered on the register of members as a shareholder. Unless this is done, the personal representative is not entitled to vote and will not count towards the *quorum*. This may mean that the company is left with only one shareholder or, if the company is a single member company, no shareholders which may cause problems (see question 12.12).

If insufficient shareholders turn up, so that a *quorum* is not established, the meeting will automatically be adjourned half an hour after the time when it was due to commence. The meeting will then stand adjourned until the same time a week later at the same place (unless the directors decide on a different time and place). If the meeting was called by the shareholders in the first place, the meeting will be automatically dissolved.

If your company's Articles are in the form of Table A and were registered prior to 22 December 1980, they will additionally provide that where a *quorum* is not present within half an hour at the adjourned meeting, the members present will constitute a *quorum* for that meeting.

8.13 What majority is needed for a resolution to be passed at a shareholders' meeting?

This will depend on the nature of the resolution. Unless the resolution falls into one of the categories below, where there are special requirements, it can be passed by a simple majority of members voting on the resolution. Such a resolution is called an 'ordinary resolution'.

Many of the more important changes that a company's shareholders are responsible for approving must be passed by a 'special resolution'. A special resolution has to be passed by 75 per cent of shareholders in a general meeting where 21 days or more notice has been given. Usually the number of votes each shareholder has will not be counted and the chairman of the meeting will simply declare the resolution carried on the strength of a show of hands. A shareholder may demand that a 'poll' is taken; if this is so, the number of votes (that is, one for each share) held by shareholders will be counted. In this situation, the majority will be ascertained by counting the number of votes cast for or against the resolution.

A special resolution is required in a number of situations including the following:

- To change a company's objects. However, shareholders with at least 15 per cent of share capital can object by applying to the court.

- To alter a company's Articles.

- To change the company's name.

- To allow a private company to re-register as a public company or *vice versa*.

- To re-register an unlimited company as a private limited company.

- To resolve not to appoint auditors where the company is dormant.

- To allow directors to ignore shareholders' pre-emption rights.

- To decide that any uncalled share capital should not be called up except on the company's winding up.

- To reduce the company's share capital subject to court approval.

- To approve the giving of financial assistance by a private company for the acquisition of its or its holding company's shares.

- To authorise the terms of a proposed contract for an off-market purchase of the company's own shares.

- To authorise the terms of a contingent purchase contract.

- To approve a payment out of capital to redeem or purchase the company's shares.

- To resolve that the company be wound up voluntarily or be wound up by the court.

Certain important company resolutions need to be passed with speed. In this event ordinary notice will suffice, but the same majority of votes is required as for a special resolution. This type of resolution is known as an 'extraordinary resolution'. Where an extraordinary resolution is to be proposed at an extraordinary general meeting, not less than 14 clear days' notice is all that is required.

An extraordinary resolution is required in the following circumstances:

- Where class rights are to be varied.

- To put the company into a voluntary winding up (where the company resolves to the effect that it cannot by reason of its liabilities continue its business and that it is advisable to wind up).

8.14 I have heard of elective resolutions – what are they?

The Companies Act 1989 introduced provisions into the Companies Act 1985 that allow private companies to elect to dispense with certain procedures. Thus, if all members agree to an elective resolution in general meeting in accordance with the statutory procedure, a private company will be able, for instance, to dispense with the holding of annual general meetings and the laying of accounts and reports. This procedure may be useful to companies where the directors and shareholders are the same persons. However, where an elective resolution to dispense with the laying of accounts is in force, copies of the financial statements must nonetheless be sent to shareholders who can, if they wish, require the company to lay accounts at a general meeting.

In addition to dispensing with the AGM and the laying of accounts, a private company can, by the elective resolution procedure, dispense with the annual appointment of auditors, reduce to not less than 90 per cent the majority required to authorise short notice of meetings, and extend the duration of directors' authority to allot shares either indefinitely or for a fixed period.

An elective resolution is not effective unless at least 21 days' written notice of the meeting is given, stating that an elective resolution is proposed and its terms. In addition, it must be agreed by all members entitled to attend and vote at the meeting, either in person or by proxy, and not just by those who attend the meeting.

A private company may also pass an elective resolution outside a general meeting by written resolution in accordance with the written resolution procedure, which is briefly described below. An elective resolution may be revoked by an ordinary resolution.

8.15 What is the written resolution procedure?

There is now a statutory procedure that permits the shareholders of a private company to agree to a resolution in writing without calling a general meeting. This means that most things that could be done by resolution of the company in general meeting, may be done by written resolution. The resolution must, however, be agreed to and signed (not necessarily on the same document) by all members of the company entitled to attend and vote at such meeting. Notice of the proposed resolution must also be given to the company's auditors.

A written resolution cannot be used to remove a director or auditor before the expiration of his period of office. There are additional conditions to be complied with where the written resolution concerns the approval of the disapplication of pre-emption rights, the funding of a director's expenditure in performing his duties, directors' contracts of employment for periods of more than five years, giving financial assistance and in connection with the purchase by a company of its own shares.

8.16 What happens after a resolution is adopted at a general meeting?

Copies of most resolutions have to be forwarded to the Registrar and recorded by him within 15 days after the resolution is passed. A copy of the resolution then has to be embodied in, or annexed to, every copy of the company's Articles issued after the resolution is passed. The resolutions to which these rules apply, are as follows:

■ Special resolutions.

■ Extraordinary resolutions.

■ Elective resolutions or resolutions revoking such resolutions.

■ Resolutions that would have been special resolutions or extraordinary resolutions if they had not otherwise been agreed by all of the members of the company.

■ Resolutions that have been agreed to by all the members of a particular class of shareholders.

■ A resolution passed to change the company's name on the direction of the Secretary of State.

- A resolution to revoke or renew an authority to the directors to allot shares or securities.

- A resolution passed by a company to alter its memorandum on ceasing to be a public company, following an acquisition of its own shares.

- A resolution conferring, varying, revoking or renewing an authority for the company to purchase its own shares where the purchase is to be a market purchase.

- A resolution for a voluntary winding up of the company.

If the company fails to file the resolutions or attach copies to the Articles, every officer who is in default is liable to a fine on summary conviction of £1,000. There is also a daily default fine of £100 for failing to file the resolutions.

Chapter 9

Your remuneration as a director

Question   *Page*

9.1   How will my remuneration as a director be determined?   125

9.2   What guidance on setting board remuneration does the
      Combined Code contain?   126

9.3   If I own the company how much can I pay myself?   126

9.4   Is there any guidance on how much directors can be paid?   127

9.5   What remuneration can I get as a non-executive director?   127

9.6   What happens if I am an employee as well as a director?   128

9.7   What about pensions and life assurance?   128

9.8   Can the shareholders find out how much I am paid?   128

9.9   What remuneration must I disclose?   129

9.10 What does 'remuneration' mean?   129

9.11 Do fees for professional services have to be disclosed?   130

9.12 What will the company disclose?   130

9.13 What other information will need to be shown?   131

9.14 My company is a small company – does it have to give the same
      information?   132

9.15 Are there any additional disclosures for listed and AIM companies required under the 1985 Act? 132

9.16 Are there any additional disclosures for listed companies required under the Stock Exchange's Listing Rules 132

Your remuneration as a director

9.1   How will my remuneration as a director be determined?

This will probably depend on the particular circumstances of your appointment, and whether you are to be a non-executive director or are to be an employee as well as a director.

A considerable amount of guidance has been published over the years on how directors' remuneration should be set. The Institute of Directors in its publication *The Remuneration of Executive Directors* considered in the context of best practice the machinery for approving executive remuneration. It says:

> *"The cardinal principle when setting board remuneration is that members should not be responsible for deciding their own pay; companies should therefore devise arrangements to prevent this. The chairman and non-executive directors, acting as a remuneration committee, could be a key element of such machinery."*

The Institute of Directors went on to say that the pay of each executive director needs to be set in relation to the responsibilities of his job relative to other appointments among his director colleagues; the market rate for the job; and his performance in position.

This and other earlier guidance on good practice in determining directors' remuneration was developed in the Cadbury and Greenbury Codes of Best Practice. These Codes are now largely incorporated into the Hampel Combined Code, which sets out the corporate governance principles and code of best practice provisions for listed companies.

9.2 What guidance on setting board remuneration does the Combined Code contain?

The Code's guidance on the subject of remuneration is that the level of remuneration should be sufficient to attract, retain and motivate the directors needed to run the company successfully. However, companies should avoid paying more than is necessary for this purpose and a proportion of remuneration should be linked to corporate and individual performance. Companies should establish a formal and transparent procedure for developing policy on executive remuneration and for fixing the remuneration packages of individual directors. Furthermore, no director, whether executive or non-executive, should be involved in deciding his or her own remuneration. By setting up remuneration committees, you can avoid potential conflicts of interest in this connection. With these principles in mind your remuneration committee should make recommendations to the board, within agreed terms of reference, on the company's remuneration policy and on specific packages for executive directors.

The Combined Code also confirms the recommendations of the Greenbury Code of Best Practice (adopted by the Listing Rules) that a company's annual report should contain a statement of remuneration policy and details of the remuneration of each director.The Stock Exchange requires the report to disclose all elements of the remuneration package of each individual director. Non-listed companies do not have to make such extensive disclosures of their directors' remuneration and are not obliged to appoint remuneration committees. But they may find the Combined Code's recommendations helpful in establishing their own remuneration policy.

9.3 If I own the company how much can I pay myself?

Even if you also own all the shares in the company, determining your remuneration is nonetheless an important issue. Subject to tax considerations and the cash requirements of the business, you will probably want to take as much out of the business you have set up as you legally can. It is important to remember, however, that the company of which you are a director is a corporate entity and separate from its shareholders and you should not, therefore, treat the company's money (or other assets) as your own.

9.4   Is there any guidance on how much directors can be paid?

The preceding paragraphs have described the corporate governance principles and provisions set out in the Combined Code. From a legal point of view there are various matters to be taken into account. For instance, a director in accepting a salary must bear in mind what the company can afford as well as what would be the going rate for the job performed by the director if he were an employee elsewhere. This is one of his duties as a director. If a director fails to appreciate this and pays himself too much, this would be relevant in assessing whether, if the company were to become insolvent, he is unfit to be a director and whether he should be disqualified. (*Secretary of State v Van Hegel [1995] 1 BCLC @ 554*). Disqualification is dealt with in chapter 13.

Minority shareholders might also have cause to feel aggrieved. They may consider that, by the directors paying themselves excessive remuneration, the company's affairs are being conducted in a manner that is unfairly prejudicial to them and petition the court under section 459 of the 1985 Act to wind the company up.

Even when there is no provision in the Articles, a director who has no service contract may be able to recover on a *quantum meruit* basis for work done for the company. Where a director has entered into a *contract for services* (for example, some consultancy arrangements) with his company, the terms of that contract will govern his remuneration. If you have entered into a contract for services this will mean that you are not employed by the company.

9.5   What remuneration can I get as a non-executive director?

The Articles of a company generally provide for the payment of directors' fees, as distinct to remuneration under a contract of service. In the absence of such a provision you have no right to be paid. Table A, Article 82, therefore, provides that *"..... the directors shall be entitled to such remuneration as the company may by ordinary resolution determine"*. The disadvantage of this is that the shareholders must agree to any increase. Table A, however, provides that a director may be reimbursed all travelling, hotel and other expenses properly incurred. Alternatively, the Articles may authorise the board to determine the level of its own remuneration, usually subject to an annual limit.

9.6 What happens if I am an employee as well as a director?

Where you are to be employed by the company under a service contract, your remuneration (which will probably include director's fees) will be governed by the terms of that contract and these terms should be approved by the board. In practice, a director in considering his remuneration will not purely be concerned with the salary payable, but will also be concerned with the entire package.

9.7 What about pensions and life assurance?

Directors should regard provision for pensions and life assurance as part of their remuneration package. As such, details of your pension entitlement may be disclosable as a separate item in the company's annual accounts if you are the highest paid director (see question 9.12). The Listing Rules require details for each director of transfer values and the increase in accrued benefits under defined benefit schemes and contributions under defined contributions schemes. In view of the different types of pension schemes and their complexity, boards wanting to set up satisfactory pension arrangements for themselves should take advice from pensions and tax experts. The subject is outside the scope of this book.

9.8 Can the shareholders find out how much I am paid?

Possibly. Depending upon your position and your company's circumstances, your company's shareholders and anyone else who obtains a copy of your company's financial statements may be able to find out some details of your remuneration. The most detailed disclosure is given by listed companies, which must disclose the amount of each element in the remuneration package of each director by name.

The remuneration that should be disclosed in the financial statements for a particular year is the remuneration receivable by you in respect of that year, regardless of when it is paid to you.

You are under a legal duty to give your company information about your remuneration so that the information can be disclosed in its financial statements. This applies even where you have been a director of a company at any time within the preceding five years. If you fail to do so, you are liable to a fine.

Furthermore, every company must keep at its registered office or principal place of business a copy of each director's service contract or a memorandum of its terms (if it is not in writing) and make such contracts available for inspection by shareholders. This does not apply, however, if the unexpired term of the contract is less than12 months.

9.9 What remuneration must I disclose?

The remuneration you are required to disclose to your company should include all amounts you are paid (and the value of non-cash benefits received) for being a director of the company whether you are paid by the company, by a subsidiary or by some third party. You cannot avoid disclosure by setting up a company in, say, the Cayman Islands, to receive the remuneration on your behalf; that would need to be disclosed as well. Nor can you avoid disclosure by getting your company to arrange for your appointment as a nominee director of a totally independent company. Your remuneration in respect of that appointment would need to be disclosed, unless you have to account for it to the company which nominated you.

A recent amendment to Schedule 6 to the Companies Act 1985 changed the disclosure for directors' emoluments to be made by private companies under the Act for financial years ending on or after 31 March 1997. The implication of these changes are considered in the questions below.

9.10 What does 'remuneration' mean?

The directors' emoluments (that is, remuneration) that have to be disclosed in the financial statements for a particular year are emoluments paid to or receivable by a director in respect of that year. This means your fees as a director and any salary received under a service contract as well as any taxable allowances, the estimated money value of any non-cash benefits and any 'golden hellos'.

The contributions that a company pays in respect of pension schemes for directors are not included in 'emoluments' for disclosure purposes.

Nevertheless, certain details regarding pension schemes for directors have to be disclosed as a separate item depending, basically, whether the scheme is a defined benefit or a money purchase scheme.

It is likely that any payment made to you will have to be disclosed as an emolument, unless you can show clearly that the payment was not in respect of your services as a director or in connection with the management of the company. When considering directors' emoluments, there is no need to distinguish between a director's service contract and a contract for services that a director has with his company. Remuneration received in either capacity will fall to be disclosed as directors' emoluments.

9.11 Do fees for professional services have to be disclosed?

Probably. It is often difficult to make a clear distinction between fees that a director receives for his services rendered to the company in a self-employed or professional capacity and remuneration for other services performed in his capacity as a director. For this reason such payments are often included with directors' remuneration rather than being disclosed as a transaction in which a director has a material interest. As to what constitutes such a transaction see question 10.13.

9.12 What will the company disclose?

The 1985 Act does not require your company's financial statements to show the remuneration you have disclosed to the company individually, unless you are the highest paid director, or, by inference, if you are the sole director. Assuming that you are a director of a private company or of a public company, which is not listed on the Stock Exchange or traded on the Alternative Investment Market, the notes to the profit and loss account will need to disclose the aggregate amount of its directors' emoluments for their services as directors or managers of the company and any of its subsidiaries for each of the following elements:

(a)   Directors' salary, fees, bonuses, benefits and expense allowances subject to UK tax.

(b)   Money or other assets paid to or receivable by directors under long-term incentive schemes (excluding shares and share options).

(c)   Company contributions to money purchase pension schemes under which the directors are accruing benefits.

Any sums you receive for accepting office as a director are treated as emoluments and will be included. Other disclosures will include the number of directors who are in money purchase pension schemes and in defined benefit pension schemes; and the number of directors who exercised share options and received shares under long-term incentive schemes.

If you are the highest paid director and the aggregate emoluments that your company discloses under (a) and (b) above is £200,000 or more, there must be disclosed separately the amounts under (a) and (b) and the pension contributions included in (c) above that are attributable to you. The company will in addition have to disclose the amount of your accrued pension under defined benefit schemes, that is, the amount, based on certain assumptions, that would be payable to you when you reach normal retirement age. It will also have to mention whether you exercised any share options and received any shares under a long-term incentive scheme.

9.13 What other information will need to be shown?

The new rules do not require companies to give the bands into which the emoluments fall, to state the chairman's emoluments or the number of directors who waived emoluments or the amount waived. However, the following amounts must, as under the old rules, still be disclosed: sums paid for accepting office as a director, sums paid to third parties for making a director's services available and the aggregate amount of compensation or damages for breach of contract paid to directors for loss of or retirement from office. In addition, the aggregate amount of excess retirement benefits under pension schemes paid to current and to past directors will need to be stated. This means that an amount need not be included if the funding of the scheme was such that the amount could be paid without recourse to additional contributions.

9.14 My company is a small company – does it have to give the same information?

If your company qualifies as a small company for a financial year it can *prepare* shorter form financial statements for shareholders under the special provisions for small companies in section 246(2) of the 1985 Act. This means that it can give less information regarding directors' emoluments.

The shorter form financial statements of a small company may disclose directors' salaries, fees, bonuses, benefits and taxable allowances, amounts received under long-term incentive schemes and company contributions to money purchase pension schemes in aggregate as one total. This is instead of having to give each aggregate individually as mentioned in question 9.12.

In addition, a small company may also take advantage of the special provisions in section 246(6) of the 1985 Act and *file* abbreviated financial statements with the Registrar of companies. Under these provisions, abbreviated financial statements need not give any of the above information regarding directors' emolument, pensions or compensation for loss of office.

9.15 Are there any additional disclosures for listed and AIM companies required under the 1985 Act?

The new rules under the Act make a distinction between listed companies (which it defines as including companies traded on the Alternative Investment Market (AIM)) and non-listed companies. Listed companies (including AIM companies) must include in the aggregate under (b) of question 9.12 the value of shares received under long-term incentive schemes. Listed companies must also give the aggregate amount of gains made by directors on the exercise of share options (including share options granted in respect of accepting office as a director).

9.16 Are there any additional disclosures for listed companies required under the Stock Exchange's Listing Rules

Listed companies (but not AIM companies) must also comply with the detailed disclosure requirements of the Listing Rules. Listed companies must now give full details of all elements in the remuneration package of each individual director by name in their annual report. This includes basic salary, annual bonuses, benefits in kind, long-term incentive schemes and share options. In addition, the company must now disclose details of the contributions to money purchase schemes paid by the company for each director and individual directors' pension entitlements under defined benefit schemes. This means that for defined benefit schemes the company must give to each director:

- Details of the increase in the accrued benefit under his pension scheme during the financial year in question.

- Details of his total pension entitlement at the end of the year.

- The transfer value.

These disclosures, which will satisfy most of the Act's requirements, are to be given in a report to shareholders by the Board.

Chapter 10

Loans to directors and other transactions

Question　　　　　　　　　　　　　　　　　　　　　　　*Page*

10.1　Can I borrow money from my company? 137

10.2　Can I get around these borrowing restrictions by setting up a
　　　subsidiary company to make me the loan? 138

10.3　Can I get a third party to lend me the money, with my
　　　company merely guaranteeing the loan? 138

10.4　I suppose then that the company cannot make a loan to a
　　　'connected person'? 139

10.5　Are there any other restrictions on public companies? 139

10.6　After all that, what is a 'loan' anyway? 140

10.7　Could this definition cover an expense advance? 140

10.8　What are 'quasi-loans' and how do they affect me? 141

10.9　What are 'credit transactions' and how do they affect me? 142

10.10　In all these situations, can't I just take out the loan, say, from
　　　my bank, and then get the company to take it over? 143

10.11　What happens if I break one of these rules about loans,
　　　quasi-loans and credit transactions? 144

10.12　How will anyone find out about these loans or other
　　　transactions? 145

10.13 Are there any rules regarding other transactions I might
       enter into? 145

10.14 What details will have to be disclosed? 146

10.15 When can I get out of having to disclose these transactions? . . 147

10.16 What happens if details of these transactions are omitted
       from my company's financial statements? 149

10.17 Are there any other disclosure requirements that affect me? . . . 149
       Under accounting standards 149
       Disclosure of controlling party 150
       Disclosure of related party transactions 150
       Under the Listing Rules 152

Loans to directors and other transactions

10.1 Can I borrow money from my company?

Generally, no. A company (whether public or private) is prohibited by the Companies Act 1985 from making loans to a director. However, there are some exceptions. The main one is that a company may make small loans to a director provided the total of such transactions does not exceed £5,000. In the case of a 'relevant company' (see question 10.4), any loans to a director's 'connected persons' have also to be taken into account in determining whether he is within this limit.

A 'connected person' is a person whom the 1985 Act regards as capable of being influenced by a director. The more important examples of the persons who are your 'connected persons' under the Act are:

- Your wife or husband.

- Your children (even if illegitimate), or step-children until they reach 18 years of age.

- A company with which you are 'associated'. Broadly speaking you are associated with a company if you and your other connected persons either are interested in at least 20 per cent of the equity share capital, or are able to exercise or control at least 20 per cent of the voting power at any general meeting.

- Any person who is a trustee where the beneficiaries of the trust include you or your connected persons as defined above, or where the trustees have a power under the trust to exercise it for the benefit of the director or the connected persons.

- Any person who is your business partner or a partner of your connected persons.

However, none of these persons above are 'connected persons' if they are also directors of the company.

The definition of 'connected person' is important and will be referred to on other occasions in this book. Decision tables to enable you to see whether loans and other transactions are prohibited by section 330 of the Companies Act 1985 are given in appendix VI.

A loan, quasi-loan, or credit transaction to a director or a person connected to him, is treated by the Companies Act 1985 as a transaction in which that director is interested. As a result, the director must disclose the nature of his interest in the transaction at a meeting of the board of directors. (See from question 5.4).

10.2 Can I get around these borrowing restrictions by setting up a subsidiary company to make me the loan?

No. A company may not make a loan to the directors of its holding company, unless it and similar loans do not exceed £5,000. But don't forget though that, subject to what is said below, a holding company may make loans to a director of its subsidiary, and that a subsidiary may make a loan to a director of a fellow subsidiary, provided they are not compensated for making the loan.

10.3 Can I get a third party to lend me the money, with my company merely guaranteeing the loan?

No. A company cannot avoid the prohibition mentioned in question 10.1 by giving a guarantee or indemnity, or by providing security, in connection with a loan a third party makes to either a director of a company, or a director of its holding company.

10.4 I suppose then that the company cannot make a loan to a 'connected person'?

Surprisingly, after what has been said above, this may be possible. An important distinction that has to be made is whether you are a director of what is termed a 'relevant' or a 'non-relevant' company. A 'relevant' company is either a public company, or a company that belongs to a group that contains a public company. All other companies are 'non-relevant' companies. For simplicity, in this chapter 'relevant' companies are referred to as 'public' companies and 'non-relevant' companies are referred to as 'private' companies. Do remember, however, that the wider definition is the correct one.

A private company may be able to make a loan to a director's connected person of any amount, provided that the director has disclosed his interest to the board and the board has power to enter into the transaction under the company's Memorandum and Articles. Such a loan is unlawful, however, if a public company makes it, regardless of its size. If your company is contemplating making such a loan, you should also bear in mind your fiduciary duties as a director (see question 5.2) and the possible legal consequences (see question 10.11).

10.5 Are there any other restrictions on public companies?

Yes. A public company is, in addition, not allowed to make a quasi-loan, enter into any guarantee, or provide any security, in connection with a third party making a loan or a quasi-loan not only to a director, but also to a director's connected person. Also, public companies cannot enter into credit transactions with directors or their connected persons. Quasi-loans and credit transactions are discussed below.

Furthermore, the exception in respect of small loans of £5,000 (see question 10.1) does not apply to loans from public companies to a director's connected person. Nor does it apply to guarantees, etc, given by public companies of the liabilities of directors or their connected persons.

10.6 After all that, what is a 'loan' anyway?

The expression 'loan' is not defined in the Companies Act 1985. However, it was interpreted in a case brought under the Companies Act 1948, where it was held that the dictionary definition of a 'loan' as a *"sum of money lent for a time to be returned in money or money's worth"* applied. [*Champagne Perrier – Jouet S.A. v. H. H. Finch Ltd.* [1982] 1 WLR 1359]

10.7 Could this definition cover an expense advance?

Quite possibly. Usually expense advances will be outside the definition above because they are not intended to be repaid, but to be used for the benefit of the company. However, circumstances may arise where the amount advanced is clearly excessive or remains unspent for an unduly long time. It may be that such an expense advance could be construed as a loan if it were contemplated that the amount should be repaid at some future time, whilst, in the meantime, the director derived a personal benefit from holding the money.

The Companies Act 1985 does, however, permit companies to provide you , as a director, with funds to meet expenditure incurred or to be incurred for the purposes of the company or to enable you to perform properly your duties as an officer of the company. A company may do this by way of loan, quasi-loan (see question 10.8) or credit transaction (see question 10.9) or any other similar arrangement. This exemption applies, however, only if one of the following two conditions is satisfied:

- The transaction has been approved in advance by the company in general meeting. At that general meeting, the purpose of the expenditure, the amount of the funds to be provided and the extent of the company's liability under the transaction must all be made known.

- It is a condition of the transaction that, if the company does not subsequently approve the transaction at or before the next annual general meeting, the director will discharge, within six months, the liability that arises under the transaction.

A public company can enter into such a transaction only if the total of such transactions does not exceed £20,000. There is no upper limit on transactions of this type in the case of private companies. It has been suggested that such transactions might include normal entertaining expenses and travel between business locations. However, excessive sums or sums that cannot be justified as necessary to meet business expenditure are likely to be loans.

Note, however, that these provisions do not restrict normal sized advances that a company makes to a director to pay for specific business expenditure. Consequently, these types of transaction are permitted without first needing to be approved in general meeting. This is because the funds the company provides to the director in this way are not lent to him.

10.8 What are 'quasi-loans' and how do they affect me?

If you are a director of a private company (see question 10.4), you will not be affected by the rules regarding quasi-loans. However, a quasi-loan also is a transaction that the law treats as one in which a director is interested, you must disclose your interest to the board. This applies to directors of public and private companies.

A 'quasi-loan' is an arrangement under which your company meets some of your financial obligations on the understanding that you will reimburse the company later.

The value of a quasi-loan is the amount, or maximum amount, that the person receiving it is liable to reimburse.

A common example of a quasi-loan arises where a director uses a company credit card to buy personal goods and he does so on the understanding that the company will settle the liability and he will reimburse the company at a later date. Another example, is the type of arrangement whereby companies in a group pay for goods and services for the personal use of a director of the holding company, on the basis that he will reimburse those companies at a later date.

Subject to the requirement for a director to declare his interest in a contract to his board, a private company may make a quasi-loan to either the company's directors or its holding company's directors, or to their connected persons. It may also guarantee or provide security in respect of a quasi-loan to such persons. However, disclosure of the transactions in the company's annual accounts will be required – see question 10.12.

A public company (see question 10.4) may make a quasi-loan to a director (but not to his connected persons) provided that the total amount of quasi-loans outstanding in favour of that director does not exceed £5,000 and provided also that he is required to repay each quasi-loan within two months. The total amount of quasi-loans will include such loans made by the company or by any of its subsidiaries to the director concerned, or, if the director is also a director of the company's holding company, by any fellow subsidiary.

Public companies are further restricted in that they are not permitted to enter into a guarantee or provide security for a quasi-loan a third party makes to either a director or his connected persons. However, where such a company is a member of a group, it is not prohibited either from making a quasi-loan to another member of that group or from entering into a guarantee or providing security for any such quasi-loan, by reason only that a director of one of the group companies is associated (see question 10.1) with another group company.

10.9 What are 'credit transactions' and how do they affect me?

If you are a director of a private company, you will not be affected by the rules in the Companies Act 1985 regarding credit transactions (see, however, question 5.4 for disclosure to the board). They will affect you if you are a director of a public company.

A 'credit transaction' is any transaction where a creditor:

■ Supplies any goods or sells any land under either a hire purchase agreement, or a conditional sale agreement.

■ Leases any land or hires any goods in return for periodic payments.

■ Disposes of land, or supplies goods or services, on the understanding that the payment (whether in a lump sum or by instalments) is to be deferred.

Note that 'services' has a very wide meaning here. It includes anything other than goods or land. The term 'land' also encompasses buildings.

A public company is prohibited from entering into credit transactions with a director except in two circumstances. It may do so provided that the total value of such transactions does not exceed £10,000. The value of a credit transaction is the price that could usually be obtained for the goods, land or services that the transaction relates to if they had been supplied in the ordinary course of the company's business and on the same terms (apart from price).

Alternatively, a public company can enter into credit transactions for *any* value as follows. It can do so where the value is not greater and the terms, on which the company enters into the credit transaction with the director, are no more favourable than the value and the terms the company would have offered to someone of similar financial standing, but who is unconnected with the company. The transaction must also have been entered into in the company's ordinary course of business.

If the value of any credit transaction cannot be ascertained, then it will be assumed to be in excess of £100,000. This means that the procedures for a 'substantial property transaction' will need to be followed (see questions 5.11 and 10.13).

10.10 In all these situations, can't I just take out the loan, say, from my bank, and then get the company to take it over?

No. Neither private nor public companies can arrange to have assigned to them, or to assume responsibility for, any rights, obligations or liabilities under loans, or quasi-loans or credit transactions (or any guarantee or security in respect of these), where the transaction concerned would have been unlawful for the company to enter into. Various ways of indirectly achieving this result are also prohibited.

An example of an 'assignment' is where you get a bank loan and subsequently your company purchases the bank's rights under the loan.

An example of an 'assumption of liabilities' would occur if your father was to guarantee a bank loan to you and subsequently your company was to arrange with your father and the bank for your father to be released from the guarantee and for the company to assume the liability on it.

10.11 What happens if I break one of these rules about loans, quasi-loans and credit transactions?

This can have serious consequences. You are likely to have entered into an illegal transaction. The civil remedy under section 341 of the 1985 Act is that the company can choose to treat the transaction as 'voidable' unless one of the following applies:

■ It is no longer possible for the cash or property involved to be restored to the company or the company has been indemnified for its loss..

■ A third party has in good faith given value to acquire rights which would be affected.

Furthermore, you will be liable to account to the company for any gain you may have made as a result and to indemnify the company for any loss or damage it may suffer. It is important to realise that, if any director authorised the illegal transaction, he, as well as the director in whose favour the illegal loan or other transaction was made, may be liable to account to the company for any gain he made, directly or indirectly, and to indemnify the company against its loss. A director who authorised the transaction will be able to avoid liability if he can show that at the time the transaction was entered into he did not know the relevant circumstances constituting the contravention.

A director of a public company may also incur criminal liability if he authorises or permits the company to enter into such a transaction knowing or having reasonable cause to believe that the company was thereby committing an offence. Conviction carries with it a maximum prison sentence of two years or a fine or both. The company, too, will be guilty of an offence, unless it did not know the relevant circumstances.

10.12 How will anyone find out about these loans or other transactions?

Broadly speaking, if your company enters into any transactions of the type discussed in this chapter with directors (or their connected parties), they must be disclosed in your company's financial statements whether they are illegal or not. In addition, the financial statements must disclose:

■ Any agreement by your company or any of its subsidiaries to enter into such loan or other transactions for a director or connected person.

■ Any other transaction or arrangement with the company or a subsidiary of it where a person who at any time during the financial year was a director of the company or its holding company has, directly or indirectly, a material interest. This also applies where a director's connected person has an interest in such a transaction. These types of transactions are considered from question 10.13.

The details that have to be disclosed are set out in question 10.14 below.

10.13 Are there any rules regarding other transactions I might enter into?

Yes. Certain transactions your company or a subsidiary enters into may require to be disclosed in the financial statements if you have a 'material' interest in them.

The Companies Act 1985 provides that an interest in a transaction is not 'material' if, where the board have considered the matter, in the board's opinion it is not material. Advice has been received that this discretionary power of the directors is unrestricted provided:

■ They do not reach a conclusion without considering the matter adequately.

■ They have come to the opinion honestly and reasonably and the conclusion is reached in good faith.

- The conclusion is not one that a board of directors acting reasonably could not have come to.

If the board have not considered the matter, the transaction cannot be presumed not to be material. There has been much discussion about the meaning of the words 'material interest'. Counsel has advised that a transaction should be considered material if it is likely to be of interest or significance to the shareholders or to the other users of the financial statements. It could be significant either because it is one of importance to the company or because it is one of importance to the director and in these circumstances it should be disclosed. However, other counsel has advised that a transaction may be material if the director's interest in the transaction is substantial.

However, the provisions of the Companies Act 1985 are complex. If you or any of your fellow directors are in any doubt about whether a director's interest is material, your company should take legal advice. In any event, the director should have disclosed to the board his interest in any contract with the company (see question 5.4).

In addition, where you either acquire a 'non-cash asset' from your company or its holding company, or dispose of a 'non-cash asset' to your company or its holding company, there are certain requirements you will have to comply with. These transactions are known as 'substantial property transactions'. A 'non-cash asset' in this context means any property, or any interest in property other than cash. Shareholders' prior approval is normally required for such transactions, unless their value at the time of the arrangement is less than £2,000 (or, if value is greater than £2,000, it is less that the lower of £100,000 and ten per cent of the company's net assets).

10.14 What details will have to be disclosed?

The following details are required by the Companies Act 1985 to be disclosed in your company's financial statements about the transactions discussed above whether they are lawful or not:

- The transaction's principal terms.

- For transactions in which a director has a material interest, the nature of the interest.

- A statement that the transaction either was made during the financial year or existed during that period.

- The director's name (as well as that of any connected person, if appropriate).

- The following details of any loan arrangement:

  - The amount of the principal and interest both at the beginning and end of the financial year.

  - The maximum amount of the liability during that period.

  - The amount of any unpaid interest.

  - The amount of any provision against non-payment.

- Similar details of any guarantee or security arrangement.

- For other types of transactions that require disclosure, the value of the transaction. For example, this requires disclosure of:

  - The amount to be reimbursed where a company buys goods on behalf of a director, or the maximum amount to be reimbursed in respect of quasi-loans (see question 10.8).

  - The arm's length value of any goods and services purchased in credit transactions (see question 10.9).

10.15 When can I get out of having to disclose these transactions?

The 1985 Act does not require disclosure in the following circumstances:

- Where the transaction is between two companies and you are a director of one company, and your interest arises only because you are also a director of the other company.

- Where the transaction was not entered into during the period in question *and* did not exist during that period.

- Where the transaction is a credit transaction, or a related guarantee or assignment and the total of such transactions outstanding at any time during the relevant accounting period did not exceed £5,000.

- Where the transaction is not a loan, quasi-loan or credit transaction but is one in which the director has an interest, where in the board's opinion, his interest is not 'material'. For this purpose, the director with an interest in the transaction is not counted as part of the board when they vote on whether the transaction is material. Note, however, that the board's opinion must be formed in good faith.

- Where a 'material' transaction involving another member of the same group is entered into in the ordinary course of business and at arm's length.

- Where a 'material' transaction would be disclosable because you have a material interest in it, but where (a) the transaction was made after the beginning of the financial year and (b) the value of the transaction did not at any time during the year amount to any more than £1,000 in total or, if it did, did not exceed the lower of £5,000 or one per cent of your company's net assets. (See question 10.13 for a discussion of what constitutes a material interest.)

- Where the transaction would be disclosable because you have a material interest in it, but only because you are 'associated' with your company (see question 10.1). No disclosure is required where your company is a member of a group and either:

  - your company is a wholly-owned subsidiary; or
  - no other group company was party to the transaction.

The result is that the exemption is available only if minority interests are not affected.

10.16 What happens if details of these transactions are omitted from my company's financial statements?

It is an offence for *any* financial statements that do not include the relevant information about transactions to be laid before a general meeting or filed with the Registrar if they do not comply with the Companies Act 1985. On trial on indictment, a director is liable to an unlimited fine or on summary trial to a £5,000 fine. The only defence you will have as a director is where you can *prove* that you took all reasonable steps to secure that the relevant requirements in respect of these transactions were complied with. Hence the importance of registering any protest you may have at a board meeting and having this recorded (see question 6.19).

Furthermore, if these disclosure requirements are not complied with, your company's auditors will have to include in their report (so far as they are reasonably able to) a statement giving the details that are omitted. In addition, auditors have certain responsibilities for considering any transactions to which the company was a party that may have been illegal or in breach of regulations. Such transactions could result in further statements in the audit report.

10.17 Are there any other disclosure requirements that affect me?

Unfortunately, yes. There are disclosures that are required by Accounting Standards and by the Listing Rules to be included in a company's financial statements.

Under accounting standards

Companies must now also comply with the related party disclosures required by accounting standards issued by the Accounting Standards Board, that is, Financial Reporting Standard 8 – Related party disclosures – (FRS 8) or the Financial Reporting Standard for Smaller Entities (FRSSE) if your company qualifies as a small company under the Companies Act 1985 and applies the FRSSE. Many transactions that are not disclosable under the Act may well be disclosable under FRS 8 or the FRSSE. These disclosures are summarised below.

Disclosure of controlling party

The name of the party controlling the company and, if different, that of the ultimate controlling party must be given. This means that, for instance, if you own or are able to exercise control over 50 per cent or more of the share capital with voting rights in a company you will be named as the controlling, or ultimate controlling party.

Disclosure of related party transactions

Companies are required to disclose in their financial statements material transactions they enter into with or on behalf of their related parties. Related party transactions include, basically, sales or purchases of goods, transfers of assets or liabilities, services given or received and finance given or received. The main exemptions from disclosure are the pension contributions actually paid to a pension fund and your emoluments as an employee of the company. Such transactions do not need to be disclosed under these standards. However, certain disclosures must still be made under the Act, see question 9.12.

A company's related parties include the company's directors and the directors of its parent company, and their close family. 'Close family' will usually include brothers, parents and adult children as well as spouses and minor children of the company's directors and those of its parent company.

The transactions to be disclosed under FRS 8 that would affect directors are similar, but generally more extensive than those under the FRSSE. However, the details of the transactions to be disclosed under both standards are the same. They both require disclosure to include:

- The names of the transacting related parties.

- A description of the relationship between parties.

- A description of the transactions.

■   The amounts involved.

■   Any other elements of the transactions necessary for an understanding of the financial statements.

■   The amounts due to or from related parties at the balance sheet date and provisions for doubtful debts due to or from such parties at that date.

■   Amounts written off in the period in respect of debts due to or from related parties.

As a consequence, details of material transactions between your company and its related parties must be disclosed in its financial statements. Some transactions with directors or persons connected with directors that are not disclosable under the Act will be disclosable under these standards. For instance:

■   FRS 8 and FRSSE require disclosure of material transactions between your company and 'close family' (including your spouse and children) who might be expected to influence or be influenced by you in their dealings with the company. This means that where your company enters into a material transaction with your adult children, brother, sister, parents or a member of your household, the transaction will generally be disclosable.

■   Under the standards, transactions that the company enters into with you or your close family in the ordinary course of its business on arm's length terms will be disclosable if material. These are generally not disclosable under the Act.

■   Under FRS 8 and FRSSE any guarantees you or your close family have given of the debts or liabilities of your company or its parent and any loans you have made to them will be disclosable.

All material transactions must be disclosed. Transactions will be material if their disclosure might reasonably be expected to influence decisions made by users of the financial statements. Materiality under FRS 8 and the FRSSE is to be judged by the transaction's significance to the company. Under FRS 8 transactions will also be material if they are of significance to the director or individual concerned. For what is considered to be material under the 1985 Act, see question 10.13

However, if your company qualifies as a small company under the 1985 Act, any abbreviated accounts which your company files at Companies House do not need to give the disclosures required by FRS 8 or the FRSSE. The financial statements prepared for shareholders will still need to give the disclosures.

Under the Listing Rules

Listed companies will, in addition, have to comply with the disclosures of transactions with related parties under chapter 11 of the Listing Rules (see question 5.13).

Chapter 11

Your shareholding

Question	*Page*

11.1   Can I own shares in my company? 155

11.2   Can I buy and sell shares in my company? 155

11.3   Do I have to notify my company if I buy or sell shares in it? .. 156

11.4   What about shares I already own when I am made a director? . 156

11.5   What 'interests' in shares must I notify? 156

11.6   What if I don't notify my company? 157

11.7   With such a wide definition of 'interests' I might not even know that I needed to notify an interest. Could I still be convicted? .. 157

11.8   Will anyone be able to find out that I have bought or sold shares in my company? 157

11.9   What is insider dealing? 158

11.10 What is inside information? 159

11.11 Who is an insider? 159

11.12 What are the penalties? 160

Your shareholding

11.1   Can I own shares in my company?

Yes. Directors of both private and public companies may own shares in their companies. In fact the Institute of Directors in its booklet, *Guidelines for Directors*, says *"The IOD favours the holding of shares by directors provided they are held as a long-term investment ..... "*.

11.2   Can I buy and sell shares in my company?

As stated above, it is desirable for directors to acquire shares in their company. Some Articles of association require directors to have qualification shares. Legally, it is permissible for directors both to buy and sell shares in their companies. The Articles of private companies will generally provide for a member wishing to transfer shares to offer them first to the existing shareholders. What you must not do, if you are a director of a listed company, is to buy call or put options in respect of listed shares or debentures in your company.

However, the purpose of directors acquiring shares is to take a personal stake in the success or failure of the business. In general, therefore, it must be undesirable for the directors to be seen to dispose of part or whole of their stake, or to deal regularly on a short-term basis. In part, this is undesirable because directors must also be assumed to have additional knowledge to that available to ordinary shareholders. Because of this, company law and the Stock Exchange require immediate notification by a listed company of details of its directors' interests in its listed shares. (See below for directors' obligations to notify dealings to the company.) The Stock Exchange also restricts directors' dealings in such shares and has set out in a Model Code (which is part of the Listing Rules) basic principles that must be complied with by directors when they deal in their listed company's shares. Directors should also be aware of the statutory provisions relating to the offence of insider dealing (see question 11.9).

11.3 Do I have to notify my company if I buy or sell shares in it?

Yes. While you are a director you must notify your company in writing of any alteration in the nature or extent of your 'interest' in its shares or debentures or those of any other group companies within five days. This means that if you buy or sell your company's shares the following will apply. You must notify your company in writing of the sale or purchase and of the number and class of shares or debentures and the company involved within five days. In calculating the five days' notice you should ignore Saturdays, Sundays and bank holidays. However, what constitutes an interest is very widely defined by the law and covers far more than simply buying and selling shares (see below).

11.4 What about shares I already own when I am made a director?

When you become a director you must notify your company in writing within five days of the existence of any 'interest' you may have in the shares or debentures of your company or any other group companies and the number of shares involved.

11.5 What 'interests' in shares must I notify?

You must notify 'interests' whether they are yours, or your spouse's or your infant children's. In general terms, most interests you have in shares will be notifiable, for example, if you are a beneficiary under a trust which holds shares in the company. There are some exclusions, however, where you need not notify, such as:

■   Options to subscribe for shares. But when a company has granted to a director a right to subscribe for shares in or debentures of the company, the company, itself, must enter the information specified by section 325 of the 1985 Act in the register of directors' interests.

■   An interest in the shares of a subsidiary where you are also a director of its holding company and the holding company is required to keep a register of directors' interests. In this case, notification given of your interest to the holding company will be sufficient.

This is a complex area. If you think that you may have an interest of any sort in the shares or debentures of your company, you should take professional advice on whether you should notify it.

11.6   What if I don't notify my company?

If you fail to notify your company of the matters above, you commit an offence and are liable on trial on indictment to be imprisoned for a maximum of two years and/or given an unlimited fine. On summary trial you can be imprisoned for a maximum of six months and/or given a fine limited to £5,000. An offence is also committed if you make a false statement in giving your notification.

11.7   With such a wide definition of 'interests' I might not even know that I needed to notify an interest. Could I still be convicted?

No. Your obligation to notify arises when you know that you have a notifiable interest or when you learn of the existence of the facts that cause an interest to be notifiable.

11.8   Will anyone be able to find out that I have bought or sold shares in my company?

Yes. All companies must maintain a register of directors' interests in shares and debentures. When your company receives your notification of an interest in its shares or debentures, it must record this in the register within three days. This register must be open for inspection by shareholders in your company without charge *and* by members of the public on payment of a fee. It must be kept either at your company's registered office or where your company's register of members is kept. If it is not kept at the registered office the company must notify the Registrar of the place where it is kept. It must be open for inspection for at least two hours a day during business hours. It must also be available for inspection at, and be accessible at, your company's AGM.

The interests in shares or debentures that are notified to your company under these rules must also be disclosed in your company's financial statements, either in the Directors' Report or in the notes to the financial statements.

Furthermore, where you are a director of a London Stock Exchange listed company your company must notify the Stock Exchange Company Announcements Office of the interest notified to it by the end of the following day. In addition, more detailed disclosure of your interest will be required in the company's financial statements.

11.9 What is insider dealing?

Insider dealing has been defined as the conscious exploitation of confidential information to make a profit or avoid a loss by dealing in securities at a price which would have been materially altered by the publication of that information. The confidence of the users of any market is vitally important for its success and this is no less the position with the Stock Exchange. Prices of securities should reflect their market value undistorted by any special knowledge of one party dealing in them. The sanctions against insider dealing are mainly criminal and it may be difficult for a person who has suffered loss to recover any compensation for it. The offences are laid down in the Part V of the Criminal Justice Act 1993.

The law is concerned with dealings in securities that are traded on the Stock Exchange or on the Alternative Investment Market. 'Securities' include shares, debentures, options and futures. Do not assume, however, that because you are a director of a private company, whose shares cannot be traded, that you need not be aware of these rules. The rules not only apply to directors, but can apply to any individual. For example, the rules may apply to you if your company has a business relationship with a company in whose shares you wish to deal.

There are a variety of ways in which a person, who is an insider, can commit the offence of insider dealing. These can be divided into three headings:

- Having price sensitive inside information, the person deals in price-affected securities.

■ Having price sensitive inside information, he encourages another to deal in such securities.

■ He discloses the information otherwise than in the proper performance of his employment, office or profession to another person.

There are two important concepts to grasp in understanding your responsibilities. These are the terms 'inside information' and 'insider'.

11.10 What is inside information?

This is specific information relating to particular securities that has not been made public and which, if it were, would have a significant effect on the price of the securities. The information would then be price sensitive information and the securities price affected securities.

The value of such information in the case of a company listed on the London Stock Exchange is usually short-lived, because such a company must in any event notify the Company Announcements Office of the Stock Exchange of any information that is necessary for shareholders and the public to appraise the company's position and to avoid a false market in its securities being created.

11.11 Who is an insider?

The rules will apply to you if you have information as an insider. A person has information as an insider if he knows it is inside information and he gets it from an inside source, where:

■ he is a director or employee of the company who issued the shares or he has access to the information from his employment, office or profession; or

■ the direct or indirect source of his information is a person mentioned above.

However, a person will not be guilty of insider dealing if he can show that he did not expect the dealing in securities to result in a profit or the avoidance of a loss; that he thought the information had been made public; or that he would have dealt in any event.

11.12 What are the penalties?

If a person is tried on indictment he could be imprisoned for up to seven years and/or given an unlimited fine. On summary trial he could be imprisoned for up to six months and/or given a fine of up to £5,000. However, a prosecution can only be brought by the Secretary of State for Trade and Industry or the Director of Public Prosecutions.

The transaction that a person has entered into in breach of the insider dealing rules will not be void or unenforceable for that reason alone.

Chapter 12

Ceasing to be a director

Question   *Page*

12.1   How long can I remain a director? 163

12.2   When should I resign from being a director? 163

12.3   Should I resign if I believe the company is insolvent? 163

12.4   How do I resign? 164

12.5   How can I retire from being a director? 164

12.6   I've seen references in financial statements to 'directors retiring by rotation'. What does this mean? 164

12.7   Can I be dismissed from being a director? 165

12.8   Is there anything I can do to protect myself? 165

12.9   Is it only the company that can dismiss me or can the board? . . 165

12.10 Am I entitled to compensation if I am dismissed? 166

12.11 Who can find out what compensation I get? 167

12.12 My company has two directors. We are the only shareholders. What happens if the other dies? 168

Chapter 12

Ceasing to be a director

12.1   How long can I remain a director?

You can be a director for as long as your company wants you to be. As stated above (see question 3.19), the Companies Act 1985 does not permit your service contract to exceed five years without being approved by the members in general meeting. Even with a service contract you can be dismissed at any time (see question 12.7). The only legal restriction on how long you can remain a director is where you are aged over 70.

The contract periods for directors of listed companies must now take account of the best practice provisions of the Combined Code. They state that there is a strong case for setting notice or contract periods at, or reducing them to, one year or less, but recognised that it might not be possible to achieve it immediately.

12.2   When should I resign from being a director?

Obviously there may be personal circumstances that will cause you to resign, such as being offered more money elsewhere, or a better job. There may be occasions when you consider resigning on a point of principle. If you do this solely as a lever in negotiations, however, you may be disappointed. Only too often has a director offered his resignation to be mortified by the chairman's brisk acceptance of it.

12.3   Should I resign if I believe the company is insolvent?

This may be the right step, but before doing so you should take legal advice. For example, you may believe that your company is incurring credit whilst insolvent and fear being held liable for fraudulent or wrongful trading, and consequent disqualification as a director (see question 13.3). In this situation, the primary defence is for you to prove that you took every step to minimise the loss to the company's creditors. It is difficult to minimise losses after you resign.

12.4 How do I resign?

You can resign as a director from the board at any time. Table A is representative of most Articles in providing that you must give notice to the company, although it does not specify what period that notice should be for. Prior to 1 July 1985, Table A used to require written notice of resignation. Resignation will be effective if notice is, for instance, given to the company secretary or the chairman. Despite the requirement of writing, if you resign orally at a general meeting of the company it will be effective if the company accepts it.

12.5 How can I retire from being a director?

Simply by following the procedure for resignation above.

12.6 I've seen references in financial statements to 'directors retiring by rotation'. What does this mean?

Table A requires all directors to retire at the company's first AGM and, further, for one third of the directors who are subject to retirement by rotation to retire at subsequent AGMs. The original purpose of this provision was to avoid boards of directors becoming self-perpetuating and to ensure that they are regularly accountable to their shareholders. Directors should retire in the order determined by their length of service since their last appointment or reappointment. Table A provides that the managing director and any executive director of a company are not subject to retirement by rotation. However, there is no bar to a director who has retired by rotation being proposed for reappointment straightaway. Under the Combined Code, it is a principle of good governance that all directors should be required to submit themselves for re-election at regular intervals and at least every three years.

These provisions in Table A are frequently an inconvenience and can easily be overlooked. Many private companies amend their Articles to remove them.

12.7 Can I be dismissed from being a director?

Yes. Your company's shareholders can remove you at any time before the end of your period of office. This is regardless of anything to the contrary that there may be in the Articles or your service contract. To propose such a resolution, a shareholder must give special notice. Your company is obliged to send you a copy of this proposed resolution, because you are entitled to speak at the meeting where the resolution is considered, whether or not you are a shareholder. In addition, you are entitled to make written representations of reasonable length, that the company must send to every shareholder who is sent notice of the meeting. You are entitled to require these to be read out at the meeting if your company receives them too late for them to be sent out to the shareholders.

12.8 Is there anything I can do to protect myself?

Yes. You can ask the shareholders to put what is called a *'Bushell v. Faith'* clause in the company's Articles. This can be achieved only in limited circumstances, and in particular, where you are not only a director but a shareholder as well. It involves the Articles being amended to give your shareholding weighted voting rights on a resolution to remove you as a director. In the case which gave rise to this clause, a company's 300 shares were held equally by three persons of whom two were also directors. The company's Articles weighted shareholders' voting rights from one per share to three per share when a resolution was put to a general meeting for the removal of the director holding those shares. The House of Lords upheld the validity of the clause.

This would not be appropriate in a public company, in particular, because the Stock Exchange would refuse a listing to a company that had such a clause in its Articles.

12.9 Is it only the company that can dismiss me or can the board?

The board cannot dismiss you, unless the Articles of your company permit this. Table A does not give the board such a power. It is, however, a common provision in the Articles of public companies, because it enables disputes to be settled with relatively little publicity.

12.10 Am I entitled to compensation if I am dismissed?

This will depend on the reason and manner of your dismissal and the terms of your service contract. If you are dismissed in breach of contract (for example, before your service contract is due to expire or without proper notice under that contract) you may be entitled to sue your company for damages as compensation for wrongful dismissal.

Where it is proposed to pay you compensation on dismissal, which is not a *bona fide* payment by way of damages for breach of contract or a pension for past services, the payment will be unlawful, unless particulars of the proposed payment (including its amount) are disclosed to the members of the company. The proposal has also to be approved by the company's shareholders at a general meeting. This also applies where such a payment is proposed as consideration for, or in connection with, your retirement from office.

The following are situations where you will not be entitled to any compensation for dismissal. These are:

■ Where you resign or retire, except possibly where the circumstances are such that your employer has committed a repudiatory breach of your service contract so that what happened is in reality your dismissal. (This is known as 'constructive dismissal'.) An extreme example of this would occur if your company was to prevent you from functioning as a director, for example, by excluding you from board meetings.

■ Where you yourself are in fundamental breach of your service contract. For example, if you were to commit a fraud or refuse to carry out your duties, you could be dismissed on the spot.

■ In certain circumstances, where your company gives you proper notice in accordance with your service contract.

Where you are also an employee of your company (see question 3.15), as you usually will be if you are an executive director, you will also have the statutory rights available to any employee who is dismissed, under the Employment Rights Act 1996. Frequently, however, the statutory compensation available, for example, for 'unfair dismissal', will not be important because of the relatively low monetary limits on what is payable. In addition, to be eligible to claim unfair dismissal, you must have have two continuous years' service. The statutory rights should not be ignored, however, because:

■   You may be entitled to an award in addition to any compensation you receive for wrongful dismissal.

■   You may be entitled to an award where you are not entitled to receive any compensation (for example, where your dismissal is 'unfair' but is not in breach of contract) or if the real reason was that you were made redundant.

Do remember though, that if you decide to pursue a claim for an award, you must comply with certain time scales. You must submit a claim for unfair dismissal to an industrial tribunal within three months of your employment being terminated, or within six months where the reason is redundancy.

12.11   Who can find out what compensation I get?

Anyone who obtains a copy of your company's financial statements can. The financial statements must disclose the total amount and nature of any compensation paid to a director or past director for loss of office. This amount must include any payment you receive in respect of the loss of any other office you held. It will, therefore, include compensation for the loss of office as director, or as manager, of any subsidiary company. The amount should also include any compensation paid either while you were a director or immediately on your ceasing to be a director. However, the amount disclosed is the aggregate of compensation payments made in one year. So if more than one director receives compensation it is not possible to ascertain the amount paid to each director other than in the broadest terms. This, however, does not to apply to the directors of listed companies where payments for breach of contract and termination payments must be given for each individual director.

In this context, 'compensation for the loss of office' includes *any* amount paid in connection with your retirement as a director, including damages for breach of contract and payments to settle claims. Because pensions are separately disclosed, they should not be included in this category of payment. But a payment into a pension scheme to augment the retiring director's benefits under the scheme should be included. Benefits in kind given to you on retirement, for example, your company car, now also have to be included. In fact, the statutory description of payments made as 'compensation for the loss of office' is widely drawn. In deciding whether a payment needs to be disclosed, you may need to take professional advice. Regard needs to be had both to the nature and circumstances of any payment rather than the description the company gives to it. For example, most *'ex gratia'* payments are *not* in fact regarded as gratuitous payments, but as payments in compensation for loss of office and therefore need to be disclosed.

12.12 My company has two directors. We are the only shareholders. What happens if the other dies?

You may have a problem. Quite how serious it is depends on whether your company is private or public.

■ *Private companies*
Although the legislation permits a private company to have a sole director, most private companies adopt Table A as their Articles. This provides that a company must have at least two directors, unless the company otherwise decides by ordinary resolution. In addition, the *quorum* required for the directors to transact business (see question 6.2) is two, unless the directors fix it at another number. Table A provides for the possibility of there being a sole continuing director. It says that he may act only to appoint another director(s) or call a general meeting of the company.

As mentioned in question 8.12 above, a private company may now have a sole member, and that member, notwithstanding anything in the Articles may constitute a *quorum*. Consequently, the sole shareholder may also be the sole director. A problem may, however, arise if the sole member, being an individual, dies. There may be no one to carry on the business if his executors do not wish to do so.

You are best advised to avoid this problem from the outset. The simplest method of doing so is to appoint a second director/shareholder.

■ *Public companies*

A public company must by law have at least two shareholders and two directors. Immediate action must, therefore, be taken if the number of shareholders or directors falls below the minimum. The Companies Act 1985 provides that if a person carries on business for more than six months knowing that the company has less than two members he will be liable personally for the company's debts during that period. To quote from Pennington's Company Law:

"A sole director of a public company cannot act in its name or on its behalf in relation to outsiders, or even in relation to members (e.g. he cannot call general meetings or authorise the registration of share transfers). Outsiders who deal with a public company unaware that it has only one director may nevertheless be able to treat the company as bound by his acts ....."

Disqualification

Question   *Page*

13.1   So what's new? Haven't directors always been
        liable to be disqualified? 173

13.2   Does the legislation apply to all directors? 173

13.3   What can I be disqualified for? 174
        Disqualification for general misconduct in connection
        with companies 174
        Disqualification for unfitness 175
        Disqualification for participation in wrongful trading 176
        Miscellaneous grounds for disqualification 176

13.4   That's a long list. Can I be disqualified for overlooking a minor
        statutory obligation? 176

13.5   What will the court take into account in assessing whether I am
        'unfit' to be a director? 177

13.6   What type of conduct might constitute unfitness? 179

13.7   Who decides whether I should be disqualified? 181
        General misconduct in connection with companies 181
        Unfitness 181
        Participation in wrongful trading 182

13.8   How long after an insolvency will it be before I know whether a
        summons will be issued against me? 182

13.9   What does disqualification mean? 182

13.10   What happens if I ignore the disqualification order? 183

13.11   Can I employ someone else to manage the company for me?   . . 183

Disqualification

13.1 So what's new? Haven't directors always been liable to be disqualified?

Yes. For some years now a court has, in certain circumstances, been able to make a disqualification order against a director; that is to say, an order that he cannot be a director of a company for a specified period of time without the leave of the court.

Liquidators and receivers of insolvent companies must make a report to the Secretary of State on the conduct of the directors of such companies if they consider the directors are unfit to be concerned in the management of a company. Such a report may be followed by an application to the court to disqualify the directors. The courts' power to disqualify is now to be found in the Company Directors Disqualification Act 1986. Companies House Annual Report for 1995-96 says that disqualification orders against directors for the year ended 31 March 1996 notified to the Secretary of State totalled nearly 1,000. This number was nearly double that for the previous year. So be alert to what follows in this chapter.

13.2 Does the legislation apply to all directors?

Yes. Any director may be disqualified if he satisfies any of the grounds for disqualification. The law expressly extends this to any person who occupies the position of a director, whatever title he is given (see paragraph 3.5). Shadow directors may also be disqualified, but only on the grounds of 'unfitness'.

You will, therefore, need to be aware of your responsibilities to avoid disqualification, even if, for example, you are a non-executive director or an alternate director, or even if you do not have the title of director at all, but are regarded as one by the law.

13.3   What can I be disqualified for?

A director can be disqualified on three basic grounds —'general misconduct in connection with companies', 'unfitness' and 'participation in wrongful trading. However, there are other miscellaneous grounds that are also mentioned below.

Disqualification for general misconduct in connection with companies

You can be disqualified by the court:

■   *On conviction for certain indictable offences*
A director may be disqualified if he is convicted of an indictable offence in connection with the promotion, formation, management, liquidation or striking off of a company, or with the receivership or management of a company's property. The maximum period for which a director can be disqualified is 15 years (five years if made by a court of summary jurisdiction).

■   *For persistent breaches of the companies' legislation*
A director may be disqualified if he is persistently in default in filing any return, financial statements or other document with the Registrar. This will be conclusively proven if he has been found guilty of three or more defaults in the five years ending with the date of the application. The maximum period of disqualification is five years.

■   *For committing fraud in the course of the winding up of a company*
A director may be disqualified if he appears to have been guilty of fraudulent trading (even if he has not been convicted for that), or has been guilty of any fraud or breach of duty in relation to his company. The maximum period of disqualification is 15 years.

■   *On summary conviction*
Where a director has been convicted of a summary offence after 15 June 1982,which relates to a breach of the companies' legislation requiring the filing of any return, financial statements or other documents with the Registrar, the court may also make a disqualification order against him in specified circumstances. These

are that to be disqualified he must have been convicted, within the previous five years, of not less than three default orders and similar offences. This applies even where the breach is not one he has committed personally, but is committed by his company. The maximum period of disqualification is five years.

Disqualification for unfitness

The court has the power to disqualify a director if it is satisfied that his conduct makes him unfit to be a director. A majority of directors of insolvent companies are disqualified on the grounds of unfitness.

A director *must* be disqualified where he is (or has been) a director of a company that has at any time become insolvent and the court is satisfied that his conduct as director makes him unfit to be concerned in the management of a company. This applies even if the company becomes insolvent after he ceases to be a director of it. In fact, not only is a person's conduct as director of the company in question relevant, but also his conduct as a director of any other company or companies. The minimum period of disqualification is two years and the maximum period is 15 years.

A company will be regarded as insolvent where either of the following applies:

- It goes into liquidation when it has insufficient assets to pay its debts, other liabilities and the winding up expenses.

- An administration order is made in respect of the company or an administrative receiver is appointed.

In *Re Sevenoaks Stationery (Retail) Limited* [1990] BCC 765, the Court of Appeal divided the permissible disqualification period of two years to 15 years in connection with unfitness into three: over ten years for particularly serious cases; two to five years for not very serious cases; and a middle bracket from six to ten years for serious cases which did not merit the top bracket. 'Unfitness' to be a director is considered further from question 13.5.

Disqualification for participation in wrongful trading

This is a very important ground for disqualification and you should refer to question 15.4 below, where liability for fraudulent and wrongful trading is dealt with.

A court may disqualify a director from being a director whenever it makes an order that he should be personally liable for a company's debts because of fraudulent or wrongful trading, even if no application for a disqualification order is made. The maximum disqualification period is 15 years.

Miscellaneous grounds for disqualification

■ It is an offence for the following to act as a director of a company without the court's permission. This extends to a director indirectly or directly taking part in or being concerned in the promotion, formation or management of a company:

   ■ An undischarged bankrupt.

   ■ A person who has failed to pay under a county court administration order.

■ Disqualification after a company investigation, on application by the Secretary of State, where it appears expedient in the public interest for a disqualification order to be made. In this instance, the court may make a disqualification order where it is satisfied that the director is unfit to be concerned in the management of a company. The maximum period of disqualification is 15 years.

13.4 That's a long list. Can I be disqualified for overlooking a minor statutory obligation?

Yes, in principle. However, the DTI, in the Guideline Notes referred to below, has stated that the 'office holder' (see below) should *"..... not take a pedantic view of isolated technical failures, e.g. the occasional lapse in filing annual returns, but should form an objective view of the director's conduct".*

It should be noted, however, that in *Re Cladrose Ltd* [1990] BCC 11 a disqualification order was made in respect of a director of three insolvent companies who failed to submit any statutory accounts or annual returns over a six-year period. The judge decided that as a chartered accountant that director was unfit to be a director (although not for any extended period) and he was disqualified for the minimum of two years. His co-director who was not an accountant was not disqualified as the judge found that his responsibility for the failure to file financial statements and returns was slight.

13.5 What will the court take into account in assessing whether I am 'unfit' to be a director?

The Company Directors Disqualification Act 1986 sets out two lists of matters that a court must in particular consider when it has to decide whether a person's conduct renders him unfit to be a director. The first list sets out those matters that apply regardless of whether the company is insolvent. The second sets out additional matters that apply where the company has become insolvent.

The first list requires the court to consider:

■   Any misfeasance (that is, unlawful act) or breach of any fiduciary or other duty by the director in relation to the company.

■   Any misapplication or retention by the director of, or any conduct by the director giving rise to an obligation to account for, any money or other property of the company.

■   The extent of the director's responsibility for the company entering into any transaction liable to be set aside as intended to defraud creditors.

■   The extent of the director's responsibility for any failure by the company to comply with the Companies Act 1985 provisions in respect of:

   ■   Keeping proper accounting records.

- Keeping the register of directors and secretaries and notifying changes to the Registrar.

- Keeping and entering up the register of members.

- Filing its annual return.

- The registration of charges it creates.

- The extent of the director's responsibility for any failure by the directors of the company to comply with the duty to prepare financial statements. This includes the provisions relating to approving and signing the balance sheet and the documents to be annexed to it.

The list is not exhaustive and the courts may consider other relevant matters.

The second list, which applies when the company has become insolvent, requires the court to consider:

- The extent of the director's responsibility for the causes of the company becoming insolvent.

- The extent of the director's responsibility for any failure by the company to supply any goods or services that have been paid for (in whole or in part).

- The extent of the director's responsibility for the company entering into any transaction or giving any preference that is liable to be set aside.

- The extent of the director's responsibility for any failure by the directors of the company to comply with the duty to call a creditors' meeting in a creditors' voluntary winding up.

- Any failure by the director to comply with the duties in relation to the company's statement of affairs, to deliver up company property, to co-operate with a liquidator, or to attend the creditors' meeting in a creditors' voluntary winding up.

13.6 What type of conduct might constitute unfitness?

Where disqualification for unfitness has been considered by the courts, the approach adopted has been broadly the same – that the primary purpose of disqualification is not to punish the individual but to protect the public. The following cases illustrated some of the principles taken into account.

No disqualification

■ In *Re Lo-Line Electric Motors Ltd & Ors* [1988] 4 BCC 415 the judge considered that ordinary commercial misjudgment is in itself not sufficient to justify disqualification. He took the view that in the normal case, the conduct complained of as meriting disqualification must display a lack of commercial probity. This line of reasoning was also followed in *Re C.U. Fittings Ltd* [1989] 5 BCC 210.

■ In *Re C.U. Fittings Ltd* the director tried to keep the company afloat in the hope that it could trade out of its difficulties. In the circumstances, the court found that the company had not used the Crown's money (in the form of unpaid PAYE tax or VAT) as working capital, but had at the relevant time been winding down its business. The director's misjudgment of the situation leading to his realisation of stock, rather than choosing to go into liquidation to preserve the preferential position of Customs & Excise, was not conduct that displayed a lack of commercial probity.

■ In *Re Wimbledon Village Restaurant Ltd* [1994] BCC 753, two directors' lapses from the required high standards demonstrated a failure to appreciate their responsibilities, which led to damage to trade creditors. They had delayed in having the financial statements audited and filed in time; thus no accurate figures were available for what was to be the company's last year of trading. Their lapses were not sufficiently serious to compel a finding that they were unfit. A third person had become a director merely to protect her unlimited guarantee of the company's overdraft, but did not take any active part in running the business. In taking this attitude she misconceived her duties as a director, being seemingly unaware of the wider responsibilities she owed to the company and its creditors. This, however, did not lead to the conclusion that she was unfit.

■ In *Secretary of State for Trade and Industry v Hickling & Ors* [1996] BCC 678, two directors should have realised that cash flow projections provided by an accountant who was the company secretary were unreliable as they had not been tested against management accounts which had not been made available to the board. However, no lack of probity was suggested and their conduct in allowing the company to continue to trade on what, with hindsight, could be seen as inadequate information was not reprehensible enough to justify a finding that either were unfit. The fact that they relied on the third person who was an accountant to keep proper accounting records, to ensure that financial statements were prepared, audited and filed did not justify a finding of unfitness.

Disqualification

■ On the other hand, in *Re Ward Sherrard Ltd* [1996] BCC 418 the directors had taken excessive remuneration after the first year's trading, had not filed audited financial statements at all and had continued to trade whilst the company was insolvent. They were disqualified for three years each. The judge found that they had a genuine belief in the future viability, but that this was not a realistic belief in the circumstances.

■ In *Re Richborough Furniture Ltd* [1996] BCC 155 two directors had caused the company to trade while insolvent, taking unwarranted risks with creditors' money and trading at the expense of moneys due to the Crown. They had misused the bank account by issuing cheques that bounced. For much of the company's life the directors did not have proper accounting records to satisfy section 221 of the Companies Act 1985 (see question 7.6). The directors were disqualified for six and three years.

■ In *Re Synthetic Technology Ltd* [1993] BCC 549, the director had procured the company to pay debts for which he was personally liable, had wrongly asserted ownership of an asset of the company in the administration and had drawn remuneration out of proportion to the company's trading success and financial health. The company had failed to file financial statements in time and had traded while insolvent, taking unwarranted risks with its creditors' money and trading at the expense of moneys due to the Crown. The court deemed this to be serious as the deficiency was large in relation to the company's capitalisation. In addition, the director had behaved in a markedly cavalier fashion with the company's creditors. He was disqualified for seven years.

13.7   Who decides whether I should be disqualified?

Ultimately, it will be the court that determines whether you should be disqualified. The procedure for this varies depending upon the grounds for disqualification in question.

General misconduct in connection with companies

An application for a disqualification order against a person for one of the grounds coming under this heading may be made by the Secretary of State for Trade and Industry or the Official Receiver.

Unfitness

Certain 'office holders' are obliged to make reports on the conduct of directors and former directors to the Secretary of State for Trade and Industry where they consider the director's conduct makes him unfit. These 'office holders' are:

- The Official Receiver.
- A liquidator.
- An administrator.
- An administrative receiver.

Where the office holder takes the view that a particular director is, in his opinion, unfit to be a director, he must give details of the conduct that makes it appear that the conditions of the legislation are fulfilled, as above. Furthermore, in submitting these reports, the office holder must have regard to the DTI Guideline Notes *Disqualification of Directors – Completion of Statutory Report and Returns.*

Where a report is made, the Secretary of State may decide to make an application (or direct the Official Receiver to do so) to the court for a disqualification order.

Participation in wrongful trading

No formal application is necessary for a disqualification order in these situations. The court that is considering the issue of fraudulent or wrongful trading will also consider whether to make a disqualification order. There has been one case where a director has been disqualified for two years at the end of wrongful trading proceedings in addition to paying damages for misfeasance. Misfeasance is discussed in question 15.4.

13.8   How long after an insolvency will it be before I know whether a summons will be issued against me?

The Secretary of State for Trade and Industry has two years from the commencement of insolvency to decide whether or not to apply for a disqualification order.

13.9   What does disqualification mean?

If a disqualification order is made against a person it means that he must not for the period specified in the order, without the leave of the court, be:

■   A company director.

■   A liquidator or administrator of a company.

■   A receiver or manager of a company's property.

■   In any way, directly or indirectly, concerned in or take part in, the promotion, formation or management of a company.

The final heading can be quite wide. The courts have held that acting as a management consultant advising on the financial management and restructuring of a company may constitute being directly or indirectly concerned in the management of a company.

13.10 What happens if I ignore the disqualification order?

First of all, if a person breaks a disqualification order he is liable to either:

- Imprisonment for up to two years and/or an unlimited fine, on conviction on indictment.

- Imprisonment for up to six months and/or a fine not exceeding £5,000, on summary conviction.

Secondly, he will be personally liable for all the 'relevant debts' of a company if at any time he breaks a disqualification order by being involved in the management of a company. The 'relevant debts' of a company are those debts and other liabilities incurred while he was involved in its management.

The law regards a person as being involved in the management of a company not just if he is a director of it, but also where he is concerned directly or indirectly with, or takes part in, its management.

13.11 Can I employ someone else to manage the company for me?

Yes, but any person who is involved in the management of a company (defined as above) and acts, or is willing to act on your instructions, without obtaining permission from a court, will also be personally liable for all the 'relevant debts' of the company. In this context, 'relevant debts' are those debts and other liabilities incurred by the company while that person acts or is willing to act on your instructions. In addition, once a person has acted on your instructions in this way, the law will treat him as willing to do so from then on, unless he can actually prove that he is not willing to. Furthermore, you would almost certainly be a shadow director of the company yourself in these circumstances (see question 3.11), and similarly liable.

Chapter 14

Company investigations

Question   *Page*

14.1   When can the Department of Trade and Industry investigate
my company? 187

14.2   What kind of investigations are there? 187

14.3   How is insider dealing investigated? 189

14.4   Are inspectors always appointed to carry out investigations? .. 189

14.5   What are the consequences of an investigation? 190

Company investigations

14.1   When can the Department of Trade and Industry investigate my company?

The majority of requests to the DTI for company investigations come from the general public. Others may be referred by the Director of Public Prosecutions, Government departments or the DTI Directorate and Agencies. A request that is formally considered may be refused if there is an adequate civil remedy available or where the police have begun criminal investigations. The Secretary of State for Trade and Industry has extensive powers to appoint inspectors to investigate and report on a company's affairs where fraud or other misconduct is suspected, on its control and on share dealings in it. In addition, he has power to require the production of documents.

The appointment of an inspector under the Companies Act 1985 is a very serious matter and tends to be restricted to large public companies. The circumstances leading to appointment are often the subject of rumour and speculation and so the public announcement of an appointment is rarely a complete surprise. The inspectors' reports are usually published if there is a public interest, but this may be delayed if criminal proceedings are being considered or are instituted.

The inspectors appointed for an investigation are usually a senior partner in a firm of chartered accountants and a lawyer (either senior counsel or a senior partner in a firm of solicitors).

14.2   What kind of investigations are there?

There are three situations in which an inspector may be appointed to carry out an investigation under the Companies Act 1985:

■　*To investigate a company's affairs under sections 431 and 432*

The Secretary of State may appoint an inspector to investigate the affairs of the company and report on them if he considers that there are circumstances suggesting that one of the following applies:

■　The company has been formed for a fraudulent or illegal purpose.

■　The company has been run so as to defraud creditors, for some other fraudulent or unlawful purpose, or in a manner that is unfairly prejudicial to shareholders.

■　Those who formed or manage the company have been found guilty of fraud, misfeasance or other misconduct towards the company or its shareholders.

■　The company's shareholders have not been given all the information that they would reasonably expect about the company's affairs.

In addition, the Secretary of State *must* appoint an inspector to investigate the affairs of the company and report on them if the court orders that a company ought to be investigated.

Furthermore, the Secretary of State *may* appoint an inspector for a similar purpose where 200 or more shareholders, or holders of one tenth of the company's issued share capital, apply for an investigation. Such applications are not common.

■　*To investigate the ownership or control of a company under section 442*

Where 200 or more shareholders or holders of one tenth of the company's issued share capital apply, the Secretary of State may appoint an inspector to determine *"the true persons who are or have been financially interested in the success or failure (real or apparent) of the company or able to control or materially influence its policy"*. The Secretary of State *cannot* refuse to order an investigation unless the application is vexatious, or refuse to investigate any particular matter unless it is unreasonable. The applicant may be required to pay up to £5,000 as security in advance and all the costs subsequently.

■   *To investigate share dealings*

The Secretary of State may appoint an inspector to investigate any circumstances that suggest to him that unlawful share dealings by directors and their families may have occurred. For example, such share dealings may include a director dealing in options in his company's shares or failing to notify his company that he has an interest in its shares (see from question 11.5).

14.3   How is insider dealing investigated?

Under section 177 of the Financial Services Act, the Secretary of State may appoint inspectors to investigate possible insider dealing offences. Inspectors are given similar powers to inspectors appointed under sections 432 or 442 of the 1985 Act. The appointment of inspectors is not usually announced and there is no power to publish their reports. Disclosure of information is permitted only in specified circumstances. The DTI Annual Report for the year ended 31 March 1997 states that 36 cases were referred to the DTI by the Stock Exchange for consideration and 21 inspectors were appointed during the year 1996/1997. As a result, two convictions were obtained and there were two acquittals during the year.

14.4   Are inspectors always appointed to carry out investigations?

No. More frequently used to investigate companies are the Secretary of State's powers to require production of documents. There are obviously circumstances where the matters of complaint regarding a company are not public knowledge and it is best for them to remain so until the facts are ascertained. On such occasions, the Secretary of State may take advantage of his power in section 447 of the 1985 Act to order an inspection of the company's books and papers. A large percentage of these investigations will invariably be carried out by officers of the DTI and will be discreet. In

1996/1997 there were 395 investigations started under section 447 covering a wide variety of types of businesses and types of misconduct.

However, the Secretary of State must have 'good reason' before using his powers in this way. If the company does not co-operate or if there is a risk of the documents being destroyed, the Secretary of State may use his powers under section 448. These enable him obtain a warrant to authorise a police officer to enter and search premises where on reasonable grounds the records are believed to be and to seize them. The investigators can also ask any past or present officer or employee to explain any records produced.

14.5 What are the consequences of an investigation?

The final product of the inspectors' investigation will obviously be their written report. This has traditionally taken some time to be published (where published). The DTI may use the information in the reports or obtained under section 447 to petition for a winding up order or for an order to disqualify the company's directors.

There may be the following consequences for a director:

■ If the investigation reveals that a director has committed a criminal offence (for example, the destruction or falsification of any document relating to his company's affairs) he may be prosecuted.

■ The Secretary of State can apply to the High Court for an order to disqualify a director (see question 13.3) where he considers that this is expedient in the public interest.

There may be the following consequences for the company concerned:

■ The Secretary of State, if he considers it expedient in the public interest, can present a petition for the company to be wound up if the court finds that that is just and equitable.

■ The Secretary of State can bring civil proceedings in the name of any company (for example, for the recovery of a company's property) where he considers that they ought to be brought in the public interest.

■ Where the Secretary of State considers that the affairs of a company have been conducted in a manner that is unfairly prejudicial to shareholders, he may make a petition on this ground to the High Court. The High Court can then make a wide variety of orders, for example to regulate the conduct of the company's affairs in the future.

In less serious cases the DTI has stated that it may take no action apart from giving the companies or directors a warning and telling them to put the faults right. You can find out more general information about company investigations from the DTI publication *Investigations: How They Work.*

Financial difficulties and company insolvency

Question   *Page*

15.1   I think that my company is in financial difficulties.
        How can I be more certain? 195

15.2   If my company is in financial difficulties, what should I do? . . 195

15.3   What alternatives are open to my company? 196

15.4   If I keep on trading what could happen? 197
        Criminal liability for fraudulent trading 197
        Personal liability for fraudulent trading 198
        Personal liability for wrongful trading 198
        Misfeasance 201
        Disqualification 201

15.5   So, what action should be taken? 201

15.6   What about an injection of capital? 202

15.7   Could I do a deal with my company's creditors? 202

15.8   Could my company be reconstructed or amalgamated? 203

15.9   What is an 'administration order'? 203

15.10   What does an 'administrator' do? 204

15.11   What will happen to me as a director when an administrator is
        appointed? 205

15.12 What is meant by 'receivership'? 205

15.13 What will happen to me as a director when a receiver
is appointed? 206

15.14 What is meant by 'voluntary winding up'? 208
Members' voluntary winding up 208
Creditors' voluntary winding up 209

15.15 What is meant by 'compulsory winding up'? 209

15.16 I've received a letter from the Registrar, saying that my company is
about to be struck off the register. What does this mean? 212

15.17 Can I apply to have my company struck off 213

15.18 May I start another company with the same name as the
company wound up? 213

Chapter 15

Financial difficulties and company insolvency

15.1 I think that my company is in financial difficulties. How can I be more certain?

As mentioned earlier in question 7.6, you and your fellow directors have a duty to keep accounting records that 'disclose with reasonable accuracy' the financial position of your company at any time. You should also be reviewing your company's progress regularly. Where management information and cash flow projections have been provided to the board on a regular basis you should be able to monitor the company's financial position and identify problems at an early stage. If these give any sign, for instance, that the company may not be able to pay its creditors on time, or faces substantial increases in overheads, they may be indicative of financial difficulties.

15.2 If my company is in financial difficulties, what should I do?

You and your co-directors must seek and obtain independent professional advice as early as possible. In the first instance, your auditors may be able to help you. In practice, unless the financial difficulties have arisen suddenly, they will be aware of your situation as they carry out their review of your financial position as part of their normal auditing procedures. Depending upon their advice, you may decide to contact a 'licensed insolvency practitioner' who specialises in administrations, receiverships or liquidations. For professional reasons, if it is necessary to appoint an office holder, for example a liquidator or receiver, he will have to be a licensed insolvency practitioner from a firm not connected with your auditors.

It is also important that you contact your company's bankers and keep them well informed of the situation. Frequently, financial difficulties arise because of temporary cash flow problems. However, a well presented case to the bank, supported by your professional advisors, may enable you to obtain an increased loan facility.

Depending upon the circumstances, it may be advisable for your creditors to be contacted to defer payment of outstanding accounts.

Although this chapter is entitled 'Financial difficulties and company insolvency', your professional advisors' first aim will be to formulate some kind of rescue plan, if that is possible and preserve the company, or a substantial part of it, in its existing form. Although in many situations this is possible, it is very important for you to remember that if there is a real risk that the company might become insolvent, leaving creditors unpaid, and if you continue to trade and incur debts, you may later be held personally liable for those debts.

15.3   What alternatives are open to my company?

First, before any informed decision can be made about the company's future, you are likely to be advised to ensure that the accounting records are up-to-date and regular management accounts are prepared. Frequently, when companies experience financial difficulties, administrative factors are neglected in favour of what happens at the 'sharp end'. One of the first considerations, if the company is experiencing cash flow problems, will be to produce short-term profit forecasts and cash flow projections. In the long-term, it may be necessary to ascertain the parts of a business's activities that are profitable and those that are not (possibly with a view to 'hiving off' the profitable parts). All possibilities will require that your professional advisors have the financial data they need to help you make an informed decision.

Secondly, it may be that, after investigating the financial position of your company thoroughly, you conclude that it is insolvent and cannot trade its way out of the situation. There are many options open to you. It is not practicable to give more than an outline of these here, but you may find the following of assistance in understanding the proposals that might be put forward by your professional advisors. Some of these options are commercial in nature, others relate to the procedures established for insolvent companies by law. Not all of these relate to the winding up of a company. The law was sweepingly revised in the Insolvency Act 1986 and the procedures established there provide a framework in which ailing companies may be able to survive. The order in which your options are laid out commences with those that will least affect your company and end with the compulsory termination of your company's life. The options are:

- An injection of capital into your company (see question 15.6).

- Arrangements with your company's creditors (see question 15.7).

- The reconstruction or amalgamation of your company (see question 15.8).

- An 'administration order' (see question 15.9).

- Receivership (see question 15.12).

- Voluntary winding up (see question 15.14).

- Compulsory winding up (see paragraph 15.15).

15.4   If I keep on trading what could happen?

This will depend upon your circumstances as outlined above. The law provides five principal sanctions against directors who, in dealing with the company's assets, act irresponsibly with regard to its creditors:

- Criminal liability for fraudulent trading.
- Personal liability for fraudulent trading.
- Personal liability for wrongful trading.
- Penalisation of directors for misfeasance.
- Disqualification.

These are dealt with in turn below.

Criminal liability for fraudulent trading

Any person who has been knowingly party to a company's fraudulent trading may at any time (regardless of whether the company ever goes into receivership, administration or liquidation) be prosecuted for this as a criminal offence. 'Fraudulent trading' here (and in the next paragraph) means carrying on the business of a company with intent to defraud its (or any other person's) creditors or for any other fraudulent purpose. This is a serious offence and applies whether or not the company is wound up. On trial on indictment the penalties are a maximum of seven years' imprisonment and/or an unlimited fine, or on summary trial a maximum of six months' imprisonment and/or a fine of up to £5,000. However, the offence of fraudulent trading is notoriously difficult to prove.

Personal liability for fraudulent trading

In addition to the criminal offence mentioned above, any person who has been knowingly party to a company's fraudulent trading may be made personally liable by the court to contribute to the company's assets, but *only* when it is in the course of winding up. It was once thought that fraudulent trading had in practice been superseded by wrongful trading (see below), but it has recently been getting a new lease of life as a few cases have been successfully brought by liquidators. The attraction of fraudulent trading to liquidators is that, if their application is successful, the courts may order damages which include a 'punitive' element as well as an amount to compensate for the appropriate trading loss.

Personal liability for wrongful trading

Under section 214 of the Insolvency Act 1986, where a company is in insolvent liquidation, the court may order a director to make contribution to the company's assets if the director knew or ought to have concluded that an insolvent liquidation was unavoidable and failed to take steps to minimise the loss to creditors. Because of its importance, the whole of that section relating to the offence of wrongful trading is reproduced in Appendix IV. As mentioned in question 5.2, in connection with a director's fiduciary duty, this section now imposes upon directors a duty to consider the interests of creditors.

In (*Re Produce Marketing Consortium Ltd.* [1989] BCLC 520) two directors (who were the only directors and only full-time employees) were held liable for wrongful trading and ordered to contribute to the company's assets to the extent that the assets were depleted by their actions. In applying the test in section 214(2) as to whether the directors knew or ought to have concluded that there was no reasonable prospect that the company would avoid going into insolvent liquidation, it was held in that case that the facts which the directors ought to have known or ascertained and the conclusions they ought to have reached were not limited to those which they, showing reasonable diligence, would have known, ascertained or reached. They included those that a person with the general knowledge, skill and experience of someone carrying out their functions would have known, ascertained or reached.

The judge went on to say that regard must be had to the functions to be carried out by the director in relation to the company. It followed, therefore, that the general knowledge, skill and experience expected of a director would be much less extensive in a small company than it would be in a large company. Nevertheless, certain minimum standards had to be assumed to be attained since a company had a statutory obligation to maintain accounting records showing its financial position and to prepare financial statements.

Section 214(4) refers to facts which a director *"ought to know or ascertain"*. In the judge's view, the factual information which a director will be treated as possessing would include not only the information that was actually there, but that which, given reasonable diligence and an appropriate level of general knowledge, skill and experience, was ascertainable. For the purposes of the test in section 214(2) the judge decided that the financial results of the company for the year ending 30 September 1985 ought to have been known at the end of July 1986, at least to the extent of the deficiency of assets over liabilities. (This is because the Companies Act 1985 gives a private company ten months after its year end in which to file accounts with the Registrar. The company's accounts for the year ending September 1985 should, therefore, have been filed by the end of July 1986.) With the knowledge that the directors were to be assumed to have of the company's financial position there would have been no alternative but to conclude there was no prospect of an insolvent liquidation being avoided. The directors should, therefore, have taken every step with a view to minimising the potential loss to the company's creditors from the end of July 1986 and not the date when they actually signed the preceding two years' accounts (that is, in February 1987). The directors had continued trading for another year after July 1986 and could not, therefore, be said to have taken any steps with a view to minimising the potential loss to the company's creditors. They were ordered to contribute £75,000 to the company's assets. Neither of the directors involved was intentionally dishonest. Wrongful trading can be seen here as the price of incompetence only.

Section 214 has the effect of placing a higher duty upon you if you possess a special skill, for example, if you are a finance director and a chartered accountant. In view of the risk of liability under section 214, if you have real doubts about your company's financial position you should make your doubts known at a board meeting and if necessary the board should take professional advice from lawyers and accountants. Failure to take immediate action may make it more difficult for you to avoid personal liability for wrongful trading.

The importance of directors being aware of their duties has again been emphasised in another wrongful trading action. In *Re DKG Contractors Ltd.* [1990] BCC 903, Mr and Mrs G, the only directors and shareholders of a company, DKG Contractors Ltd, were found liable for wrongful trading and ordered to contribute £417,000 to the company's assets. This represented trading losses from the date when Mr. and Mrs. G should have known there was no reasonable prospect of avoiding liquidation. This date was, in the judge's view, when creditors were pressing and a supplier refused to make deliveries. In another wrongful trading case, *Re Purpoint Ltd* [1991] BCC 121, the date on which it should have been plain to the directors that the company could not avoid going into insolvent liquidation was the date when the company could not meet its trade debts as they fell due and owed very large amounts of PAYE and NIC which it had no prospect of paying.

The directors in *Re DKG Contractors Ltd* (mentioned above) had also made payments (that amounted to wrongful preferences) to Mr G (who was also a creditor) at a time when the company was unable to pay its debts, with a view to putting him in a better position in the event of liquidation than he would have been in otherwise. The judge accepted that neither of the directors knew much about companies and that Mr G, in particular, had no real idea what being a director entailed. However, he made no attempt to find out what his duties as a director might be. Mrs G had only limited previous experience of bookkeeping. The judge considered that whilst neither Mr or Mrs G acted dishonestly, they had not acted reasonably and consequently ought not to be excused from personal liability.

Misfeasance

The Insolvency Act 1986 gives a liquidator a remedy against directors who have misapplied or retained or become accountable for any money or other property of the company. Misfeasance does not necessarily involve dishonesty, but includes any breach of duty involving a misapplication of assets or wrongful detention of the company's monies. Examples are: payment of dividends out of capital; sale of assets at an undervalue; or directors making a secret profit. The court may examine the conduct of the directors and compel them to repay or restore the money or the property with interest, or contribute money to the assets by way of compensation. In *Re Purpoint Limited* (referred to above) a director was found liable for wrongful trading and misfeasance. The judge ordered the director to pay compensation to the liquidator, because the director had bought an unnecessary capital asset (that is, a car for his own use) with company money and had withdrawn cash sums from the company which were unaccounted for.

Disqualification

A person, whether an executive or non-executive director, who is responsible for fraudulent or wrongful trading may be disqualified (see question 13.3). Several examples of disqualification have already been given in chapter 13.

15.5   So, what action should be taken?

Whenever wrongful trading is an issue, the golden rule is to take proper professional advice as soon as possible. Auditors are seldom qualified to give that advice. You should consider involving a licensed insolvency practitioner, who could be an accountant or solicitor who specialises in insolvency work and has been granted a licence by his professional body. The action will, therefore, depend on the advice you receive from your advisers and whether their view is that the company's financial difficulties stem from temporary cash flow difficulties or whether the difficulties are more serious. Some possible courses of action are set out below.

If the difficulties are serious, your advisers may consider it appropriate for the company to have an administrator or receiver appointed (to give it a chance of survival) rather than immediately to seek its winding up. They could, therefore, suggest that the company or the directors apply to the court for an administration order under Part II of the Insolvency Act 1986. Whilst an administration order is in force no order may be made for winding up the company, the company's secured creditors cannot take any steps to enforce any security, and no legal proceedings can be started or continued without the leave of the court. This gives the company a breathing space to enable the administrator appointed as a result of the administration order to draw up his proposals for the company's future. Alternatively, if your company has granted a floating charge over its assets your advisers may suggest that the directors should invite the holders to appoint an administrative receiver. More information about receivers and administrators is included in questions 15.9 to 15.12 below.

15.6   What about an injection of capital?

Very often a company finds itself in difficulties because of cash flow problems even though, technically, it is quite solvent. In such circumstances the answer may be to obtain external finance. The terms upon which such capital is received should be considered in close consultation with your professional advisers. For example, will the provider of the capital want to take an equity share in your company?

15.7   Could I do a deal with my company's creditors?

Again, where a company's financial difficulties stem from temporary cash flow difficulties, your advisers may suggest that the company should try to come to an arrangement with its creditors. The Insolvency Act 1986 has introduced a method of compromise with creditors known as a 'voluntary arrangement', which is conducted under the supervision of an insolvency practitioner. This involves the agreement of the shareholders and creditors to the directors' proposals to keep the company in existence, generally by restructuring its debts. A disadvantage is that it is sometimes difficult to obtain the agreement of secured creditors. In addition, this may not be a sufficient course of action if your company is insolvent or likely to become insolvent in the near future. Consequently, proposals for voluntary arrangements are often made during a liquidation, or whilst an administration order is in force where the rights of secured creditors are restricted.

15.8 Could my company be reconstructed or amalgamated?

A form of internal reorganisation of your company may be advisable. The Companies Act 1985 section 425 provides a procedure under which a company, its creditors, the liquidator (in a winding up) or the administrator (where an administration order is in force) may put forward proposals for a compromise or arrangement, which then has to be approved by the court. When approved it is binding on all parties. Alternatively, section 110 of the Insolvency Act 1986 gives power to a company to reconstruct by means of a voluntary liquidation and for the liquidator to seek the sanction of shareholders to the transfer of the assets of the company to a new company in exchange for shares or other securities of the new company.

A similar process may be employed by a receiver known as 'hiving down'. The receiver sells the assets under his control to a new company set up for the purpose. The shares in the new company are then held by nominees of the receiver in trust for the old company. The advantage of this procedure is that the new company can be sold more easily.

An amalgamation of your company takes place where your company merges with another. You will, however, need to take legal advice before embarking on a reconstruction or amalgamation.

15.9 What is an 'administration order'?

As noted above, you may be liable for wrongful trading, unless you can show that you have taken every step with a view to minimising the potential loss to your company's creditors. One way that you can do this is to petition the court for an administration order. In fact, your company's shareholders and creditors can also do this. An administration order is an order directing that for a specified period the affairs, business and property of the company is to be managed by an administrator appointed for the purpose by the court.

An administrator, who must be a licensed insolvency practitioner, acts in a similar way to the traditional receiver (see question 15.10) of a company who is usually appointed by a bank to manage a business until a debenture is repaid. In fact, it was the success of that procedure that has led to the introduction of the administration procedure, that can operate where there is no debenture holder to appoint a receiver.

To obtain an administration order appointing an administrator you must satisfy the court that the company is, or is likely to become, unable to pay its debts, but is not in liquidation. The court can make an order only if it considers it likely to achieve one or more of the following purposes:

- The survival of the company, and the whole or any part of the business, as a going concern.

- The approval of a voluntary arrangement with creditors (see question 15.7).

- Compromise or settlement with creditors.

- A more advantageous realisation of the company's assets than there would be if the company were wound up.

Administrations however, are rare, affecting between 1 per cent and 2 per cent of all company failures. Because they are very expensive to implement they are outside the budget of most insolvent companies.

15.10 What does an 'administrator' do?

On his appointment, an administrator must take control of the company's property. He must prepare proposals that show how the purposes specified in the administration order can be achieved. A formal statement of these must be made to the court within three months. In practice, commercial reasons dictate a shorter period. This statement has to be given to the company's shareholders, creditors, and the Registrar. A meeting of creditors must be called to consider the proposals. If they are approved, the administrator will be required to manage the affairs, business and property of the company in accordance with those proposals. To do this he is given power to *"..... do all such things as may be necessary for the management of the affairs, business and property of the company"*. A long list of particular powers is given in the Insolvency Act 1986.

15.11 What will happen to me as a director when an administrator is appointed?

You will remain a director, although you can exercise your powers only in such a way that will not interfere with the administrator. You may be dismissed by the administrator. The administrator can also appoint directors. The administrator must report on any unfit director to the Secretary of State for Trade and Industry, and this may result in a disqualification order being made (see question 13.7). When the administrator has achieved his purposes he must apply for a court order to discharge him. If you are still a director, unless the company is wound up, you will then be able to exercise all your powers as you did before the order was made.

15.12 What is meant by 'receivership'?

It is common for a major creditor, usually the company's bank, to require the company to give it security for the monies owing under overdraft or other facilities. This security may be in the form of a 'debenture' or 'debenture deed'. A common type of debenture creates what is called a 'floating charge'. It 'floats' in that it is a charge on both the present and future assets of your company, whatever they may be. The debenture deed specifies particular events, such as default on repayment of a loan, that will terminate your permission to deal with the assets subject to the charge and entitle the debenture holder to appoint a receiver. This is called the 'crystallisation' of the charge. Another type of charge is a 'fixed charge' that relates to specified assets only, such as your company's land and buildings. A debenture may incorporate both fixed and floating charges and banks' debentures usually do.

A debenture will usually entitle its holder to the appointment of a receiver in the following circumstances:

- Where your company fails to repay the monies secured by the debenture.

- Where your company exceeds its debenture trust deed's borrowing limits and does not comply with notices requiring a reduction in borrowing.

- Other breaches of the debenture deed.

- At the request of the directors.

The receiver (called an 'administrative receiver' in the case of a floating charge or a fixed and floating charge over all the company's assets) must be a licensed insolvency practitioner. A person appointed purely under a floating charge over part only of the assets is merely called a 'receiver' and, surprisingly, does not need to be a licensed insolvency practitioner. He is appointed as an individual even though he may be a partner in, for example, a firm of chartered accountants.

The purpose of an administrative receiver's appointment is for him to take control of the charged assets with a view to paying off the liability to the debenture holder, although he must pay off any 'preferential debts' first.

15.13 What will happen to me as a director when a receiver is appointed?

You will be in a very similar position to that where an administrator is appointed (see question 15.11), although, depending upon the terms of the debenture, your powers may be less restricted. Most important of all, as soon as a receiver is appointed you will no longer have the authority to deal with the property charged under the debenture. Where there is a floating charge this will effectively divest you of any real authority within your company. In contrast to the position where an administrator is appointed, however, a receiver does not have the power to dismiss you as a director.

You must remember, however, that although you are divested of many of your powers as a director, you are still subject to the same obligations as before, for example, to file an annual return with the Registrar.

Like an administrator, an administrative receiver is under a duty to report on any unfit director to the Secretary of State for Trade and Industry, which may result in a disqualification order being made (see question 13.7).

Frequently, receivership leads to a company's liquidation or winding up (see question 15.14). However, if a receiver is able to pay off the amount secured by the debenture and has given notice to the Registrar that he has ceased to act, you will continue to be a director with full powers as before.

15.14 What is meant by 'voluntary winding up'?

If your company is in financial difficulties, yet is solvent in that it could pay its debts in full by selling its assets, it may be advantageous to consider a voluntary winding up. An orderly winding up will invariably realise a higher value for assets than a forced sale.

A voluntary winding up is commenced when the shareholders of a company adopt a resolution for their company to be wound up. The principal types of voluntary winding up are known as either a 'members' voluntary winding up' or a 'creditors' voluntary winding up'. The liquidation will proceed as a members' voluntary winding up provided that a majority of the board of directors make a statutory declaration of the company's solvency within five weeks before the adoption of the winding up resolution. Otherwise the winding up will have to proceed as a creditors' voluntary winding up.

Members' voluntary winding up

The statutory declaration has to state that the directors making it have made a full enquiry into the affairs of the company and have formed the opinion that the company will be able to pay its debts in full, together with interest, within a specified period that must not exceed 12 months from the commencement of the winding up. The statutory declaration must include a statement of the company's assets and liabilities at the latest practicable date before it is made. As a director, you should consider very carefully whether or not to make such a declaration. If the company's debts are not paid or provided for within the period stated those who made the statement will be presumed by the law *not to* have had reasonable grounds for making it. Furthermore, any director who makes the statutory declaration without having reasonable grounds for the opinion expressed in it, commits a criminal offence. This is punishable with imprisonment for up to two years and/or an unlimited fine on trial on indictment or to a maximum of six months' imprisonment and/or a fine of a maximum of £5,000 on summary trial.

The shareholders will usually appoint a liquidator at the general meeting at which the winding up resolution is adopted. No notice is required to propose the appointment. This is important because, until a liquidator is appointed, after the resolution the directors commit an offence if they continue to exercise their powers. The appointment of a liquidator will usually bring your powers as a director to an end, other than for the purpose of protecting the assets, although the shareholders or the liquidator may permit you to exercise some or all of your powers.

The liquidator will act to realise all the company's assets and distribute the proceeds to creditors and shareholders, subject to his own costs. If at any time he comes to the opinion that the company will not be able to pay its debts in full within the stated period, he must call a meeting of the company's creditors and the winding up will become a creditors' voluntary winding up.

Creditors' voluntary winding up

If a creditors' voluntary winding up comes about for one of the reasons above, there are certain consequences. The liquidator must hold a creditors' meeting that will decide whether to appoint a liquidator in place of himself, because he was appointed by the shareholders. If, however, a resolution is passed for a voluntary winding up and the directors have not made a declaration of solvency, the company must call a creditors' meeting within 14 days. A liquidator will be appointed by the creditors at this meeting. There are various publicity requirements that attempt to ensure that creditors are aware of the opportunity to exercise their votes. At the creditors' meeting the creditors may decide to appoint a liquidation committee to assist the liquidator and to receive reports on the progress of the liquidation.

The procedure for the final dissolution of the company, once the liquidator has realised the company's assets and completed the necessary distribution, is considered in question 15.15.

About 60 per cent of insolvent liquidations are voluntary, rather than compulsory windings-up. The process is slightly less onerous for directors and shows their creditors that they have taken the decision themselves to stop trading.

15.15 What is meant by 'compulsory winding up'?

The meaning of 'winding up' has been considered above in the context of voluntary winding up. Those persons who may present a petition before a court seeking the compulsory winding up of a company are:

■ The company.

■ The company's directors.

■ The Secretary of State for Trade and Industry.

■ A contributory (usually meaning a shareholder). (In legal terms, this means a person liable to contribute to the assets of the company if it is wound up. Shareholders are only liable for the amounts unpaid on their shares.)

■ A creditor.

■ An official receiver (for companies only registered in England and Wales, as there is no official receiver in Scotland).

■ An administrative receiver, administrator or supervisor.

The grounds on which a company may be wound up by the court are as follows:

■ The company has passed a special resolution that it be wound up by the court.

■ It is a public company and a year or more has expired without it obtaining a certificate relating to compliance with its share capital requirements (see appendix I).

■ The company does not commence business within a year of its incorporation or suspends business for a year.

- In the case of a public company, the number of shareholders is reduced below two (see appendix I).

- The company is unable to pay its debts. This is the most common ground where a creditor petitions for a company's winding up. A company is deemed to be unable to pay its debts primarily where a creditor owed more than £750 has served a written demand on a prescribed form requiring the company to pay the sum due and the company fails to pay it within three weeks.

- The court considers it just and equitable that the company should be wound up. This ground is often used in small companies, that are essentially a partnership in corporate form, where there is an irreconcilable difference of opinion between the 'partners'.

The procedure for a compulsory winding up usually commences when a creditor presents a petition to the County Court (where the company's paid up share capital does not exceed £120,000) or to the Chancery Division of the High Court. A copy of the petition is served at the company's registered office and a date will be fixed for the petition to be heard. There are various publicity requirements and, in addition, the creditor has to file an affidavit with the court. However, the court may at any time before making of a winding up order, appoint a provisional liquidator. The purpose of the appointment is to preserve the company's assets where there is the danger that they may be dissipated. Such an appointment effectively takes away the directors' powers, although they retain a power to apply to the court to discharge the order. For obvious reasons, the application has to be made *ex parte,* that is, without the company being a party, which means that the company will not have an opportunity to put its side of the case. As a consequence, the court will invariably require an undertaking from the petitioner that he will compensate the company for any loss it suffers if winding up is not subsequently ordered.

On the assumption that the petition is granted by the court, the official receiver will be appointed as provisional liquidator to take custody of the company's assets. The official receiver is appointed by the Secretary of State for Trade and Industry and each court in England and Wales that has jurisdiction in insolvency has one or more official receivers attached to it.

Their main task is to investigate the causes of insolvencies and to act as a liquidator in compulsory liquidations. Within 12 weeks of the winding up order the official receiver may call separate meetings of creditors and contributories to decide whether an application should be made to the court for someone other than the official receiver to be appointed as the liquidator. Alternatively, the official receiver may apply himself to the Secretary of State for Trade and Industry to appoint a liquidator. There are various publicity requirements in respect of those meetings.

Insolvency practitioners, usually acting as part of a firm of chartered accountants, will generally accept appointment as liquidator only where a company has sufficient assets to pay their fees. However, most will be willing to attend creditors' meetings on behalf of creditors free of charge in the hope that they will be appointed liquidator. Where a company has few assets, it will not usually be worthwhile appointing a liquidator (if one could be found willing to be appointed) and the official receiver will act as liquidator. This occurs in the majority of cases.

In contrast to the position in a voluntary winding up, the law does not expressly provide that your powers as a director cease on the appointment of a liquidator. However, the extensive powers of a liquidator will leave you with little role. For example, the liquidator is under a duty to take into his custody or control all the company's property.

The law places a duty on a number of persons, including the company's officers, directors, company secretary and auditor to give the liquidator such information concerning the company as he reasonably requires and also to attend upon him at such times as he may reasonably require. You cannot escape this by resigning; it applies to those who have been officers of the company at any time. Employees are also under this obligation. It is a criminal offence to fail to comply.

When the liquidator has realised all the company's assets and completed the distributions necessary he will send a summary of receipts and payments to the creditors and contributories with a notice that he intends to apply for his release. He will then send a final account to the DTI. The liquidator must summon a final creditors' meeting when it appears to him that the winding up is complete for all practical purposes. He then notifies the Registrar that the final meeting has been held. On receipt of that notice the Registrar must complete various publicity requirements and after three months the company will be dissolved.

15.16 I've received a letter from the Registrar, saying that my company is about to be struck off the register. What does this mean?

This probably means that you have not filed an annual return or some other document required by the Companies Act 1985 for some time and have ignored various reminders.

The procedure for striking companies off the register works in the following way. If the Registrar has reasonable cause to believe that a company is not carrying on business (for example, because it fails to file any documents or reply to correspondence) he will write to the company enquiring whether it is in operation. If he receives no reply to this he sends a warning letter, such as you have received. If you do not reply to this he will issue a notice in the *London Gazette* (in the case of a company registered in England and Wales) and send you a copy. The notice will state that the company will be struck off the register (unless a reason is shown for it not to be) three months from the date of the notice. If your company has been struck off the register by this procedure, it can be restored. However, you should seek professional advice on how to achieve this.

15.17 Can I apply to have my company struck off?

The Companies Act 1985 now provides a procedure under which a company that has not traded for at least three months may apply to the Registrar to have its name struck off the register. However, this procedure imposes some onerous duties on you as a director. These include the following. The application must be made by the directors or a majority of them to the Registrar on Form 652a. This form requires them to state that the company has not, for the past three months, traded or carried on business, changed its name, sold any property it would have sold in the normal course of trading or engaged in any other activity. The Registrar will publish a notice of the application to strike off in the Gazette inviting any person to give reason why he should not do so. In addition, the directors must send a copy of the application, within seven days, to all members, employees, creditors and other directors of the company and to the trustees of any employee pension fund. Failure to do so is an offence.

There are, however, various disadvantages about the procedure. For instance, it cannot be used where the company is already being wound up, where there is a receiver or manager of the company's property or an administration order is in force. On dissolution any assets that remain in the company will be forfeited as *bona vacantia*, generally to the Crown. Furthermore, any liability that you may have as a director or shareholder before dissolution may be enforced as if the company had not been dissolved.

15.18 May I start another company with the same name as the company wound up?

You will generally not be able to do so if the company whose name you wish to use was insolvent when it was wound up and you were a director of it. The law prohibits the use of the name of a company that went into insolvent liquidation. This applies to a person who was a director (or shadow director) of that company at any time during the twelve months before liquidation. The prohibition applies for five years, unless the person has the consent of the court to be a director of a company with a prohibited name and to be concerned with the management of such a company. A person who does not comply with these provisions will be committing an offence. It was held in a recent case that the offence is one of strict liability. This means that it is not necessary for the prosecution to prove that the director(s) concerned had intended anyone to be deceived or confused in any way (*R v Cole & Others* [1997] 8 Current Law para 339).

Why set up a company?

(i) What are the advantages and disadvantages of setting up a company?

Advantages

Limited liability

There can be little doubt that the majority of people who set up a company to carry on a business do so to obtain the advantage of limiting their liability for the debts and obligations of the business to the amount they contribute as capital on forming the company.

In contrast, if you trade on your own account you are *always* personally liable for the debts and obligations you incur. Alternatively, if you carry on business in partnership with others you are *always* jointly liable with your other partners for the debts and obligations of the partnership. So there is, therefore, a real advantage in obtaining limited liability through incorporating your business as a company.

However, there are a number of situations where the protection of limited liability can be lost, for example:

■   Where a company's bankers or other creditors require a personal guarantee from its directors as a condition of giving the company finance, or of trading with it (see question 3.21).

■   Where a director or shareholder is made liable to contribute to the assets of a company, because of fraudulent or wrongful trading (see question 15.4).

■ Where a director is involved in the management of a company in contravention of a disqualification order (see question 13.10).

■ Where a director has misapplied company assets or been guilty of breach of fiduciary duty, the liquidator may apply to the court for an order compelling the director to repay or restore the assets or compensate the company for its loss (see question 15.4).

Commercial acceptability

If you incorporate a business you will frequently find that a company is more readily accepted by other businesses you wish to deal with. The reason for this is that the law governing companies is strict (for example, in relation to the audit requirement) and it is possible to find out far more about a company than about a sole trader or partnership.

Expansion

Because of the problems of personal liability, and the difficulties of obtaining finance, it is hard for a person trading on his own account to expand his business beyond a certain point. Even by entering into partnership with others these problems cannot wholly be overcome, because the Companies Act 1985 prohibits the formation of trading partnerships that have more than 20 partners. There are specific exemptions for solicitors and accountants and other professional partnerships.

The company is an ideal vehicle for business expansion. Apart from there being no limit on the size of a company, the separation of ownership from management enables the owners of shares to sell their interest in the business in a relatively straightforward manner. Furthermore, a public company can market its shares to the public, provided that stringent conditions of the Stock Exchange are complied with, enabling the company to raise very large sums of finance.

Continuity

A company as a person will be legally unaffected by changes in its membership whether by death or transfer. Changes in a partnership will often bring about its dissolution and this can be administratively very inconvenient.

Taxation

Although the effects of taxation are not considered in this book there are occasions where carrying on business may be more advantageous *via* a company. This is a question on which professional advice should always be taken.

Disadvantages

The main disadvantages you should consider before setting up a company are the burden of regulation under company law upon those running it and the publicity that must be given to its affairs. This is in contrast to the lesser regulation and greater privacy relating to their financial affairs enjoyed by sole traders and partnerships. Such regulation is not just an inconvenience, but can also be costly in financial terms. You should not necessarily let this discourage you, however, from carrying on a business through a company. Much of the legislation that places a burden upon companies (for example, VAT and employment rules) applies equally to sole traders and partnerships.

Where you will be a director as well as a shareholder after setting up a company, you will take on major responsibilities. It is with these responsibilities that the main part of this book is concerned.

(ii) How is a company formed?

The procedure which follows below is that used to form a private company limited by shares (the most common type of company formed). Other types of company may be formed and those are considered in paragraph (iii) of this Appendix.

In practice, most companies are formed by specialised company formation agents and purchased 'off-the-shelf'. This method of formation is convenient and quick and your professional advisors should be able to assist you in the process. The cost of buying an off-the-shelf company will usually be in the region of £200 to £300 (excluding any professional fees involved).

Occasionally, there may be reasons why an off-the-shelf company is not suitable, for example, if you wish to include special provisions in the Memorandum or Articles of association.

To form a private company you need to send to the Registrar of companies the following:

- The Memorandum of association (see question 2.3).

- The Articles of association (if Table A is not to be adopted) (see question 2.4).

- Form 10 (The statement of first directors and secretary and intended situation of the registered office). This names the people who have agreed to act as the company's first directors and secretary (together with their written consent) and gives the location of the company's registered office (see question 2.7).

- Form 12 (The declaration of compliance with the statutory requirements of the Companies Act 1985). This is a statutory declaration stating that the requirements of the Companies Act 1985 have been complied with. It is made either by the solicitor engaged in the formation of the company or by a director or the company secretary named.

- A fee, currently of £20 or, if a same day incorporation is required, of £100.

Where the registered office of the company is to be in England or Wales the documents should be sent to the Registrar of companies for England and Wales. Where the registered office of the company is to be in Scotland, the documents should be sent to the Registrar of companies for Scotland. The Registrars are appointed by the Secretary of State for Trade and Industry and have statutory duties and powers relating to the registration of companies and the receipt, examination, filing and making available of a wide range of documents that companies are required to provide under company law. The Registrar of companies for England and Wales is also chief executive of Companies House, an executive agency within the Department of Trade and Industry, whose main functions include the registration of new companies and registration of information about companies.

Provided that these documents are in order, the Registrar of companies will issue a certificate of incorporation. The company then exists from the date given on the certificate.

(iii) What are the different types of company?

Company law has given rise to a large number of classifications of companies depending, for example, on their size and purpose. There are four basic types of company:

Private companies limited by shares

The distinguishing feature of these companies is that their names must end with the word 'Limited', although this can be abbreviated to 'ltd'. A company which has its registered office in Wales can use the Welsh equivalent, 'cyfyngedig' or 'cyf'. There is no minimum share capital and it is usual for there to be at least two members. However, since 15 July 1992, it has been possible for a private company limited by shares or guarantee to be formed by one person and to have a single member.

Private companies limited by guarantee without a share capital

These companies are formed in basically the same way as other private companies and in general are subject to the same legal rules. They are usually formed for charitable, social or other non-trading purposes. Schools and colleges, professional and trade associations, clubs and management companies for blocks of flats are commonly established in this way.

The distinguishing features of such companies are:

■ They may omit the word 'Limited' from their name, provided that they fulfil certain conditions, including an application to the Registrar of companies.

■ They have no share capital. Each member of the company instead has to undertake in the Memorandum of association to contribute to the assets of the company if it is wound up. The extent of this guarantee is usually only £1.

■ The Articles of association, although based on Table A, are amended and can be found in SI 1985/805 Table C.

Public companies limited by shares

These companies are smaller in number and tend to be larger than private companies. They must, however, have at least two members. Public company status is a precondition to a company applying for a London Stock Exchange listing. Provided that certain conditions and procedures are followed, a private company may re-register as a public company.

The distinguishing features of such companies are:

■ The Memorandum of association must state that the company is to be a public company.

■ The name of the company must end with the words 'public limited company' which may be abbreviated to 'p.l.c'. If the Memorandum of association states that the company's registered office is to be in Wales, the name may alternatively end with the words 'cwmni cyfyngedig cyhoeddus', which may be abbreviated to 'c.c.c'.

■ A public company may, provided that it satisfies various conditions, offer its shares to the public.

■ A public company, once it has been incorporated, must not do business or borrow unless the Registrar of companies has issued it with a trading certificate. This certificate cannot be obtained, unless a director or the secretary of the company has filed a statutory declaration on Form 117 with the Registrar of companies. This declaration must state that the nominal value of the company's allotted share capital is no less than £50,000. Because only a quarter of this needs to be paid up, a public company can in fact be set up with a paid up capital of only £12,500.

There are a variety of legal rules applicable to public companies that do not apply to private companies. However, these differences are outside the scope of this book.

Unlimited companies

As the name suggests, an unlimited company is one where the members will be required to contribute their assets to the company in a winding up to the extent that the company cannot pay its debts. As mentioned in paragraph (i) of this appendix, the protection of limited liability can be illusory in certain circumstances. In some situations there is advantage in setting up an unlimited company (for example, an unlimited company does not need to file its financial statements with the Registrar of companies, unless it is a subsidiary of a limited company). As a result, the financial statements of many unlimited companies are not open for public inspection.

Your responsibilities to your employees

(i)   Who exactly are my company's employees?

You may think that the answer should be obvious. However, the law recognises an important distinction between people engaged under contracts of service – employees – and those engaged under contracts for services – perhaps described as consultants or the self-employed. This distinction is not of mere academic interest. If a person performs work for you as an employee, he will be entitled to a wide variety of statutory rights and you will owe him corresponding obligations, in addition to those under his contract. Your non-contractual obligations to the self-employed, on the other hand, are less onerous, although certain statutory requirements do extend to many self-employed staff. These include providing a safe place and system of work, the anti-discrimination laws and the rules governing working time that apply from 1 October 1998, such as the right to paid holiday. Furthermore, the operation of the taxation system applies differently for the employed and self-employed. An employer has an obligation to deduct tax under the PAYE scheme for his employees whereas self-employed workers are responsible for their own tax affairs. Social security contributions also operate differently.

There are a number of factors to be taken into account when deciding whether a person is an employee or is self-employed. The important point to remember is that you cannot get out of your legal obligations to an employee simply by calling him 'self-employed'. It is the substance of the relationship and not its form that the Courts will look at.

Factors considered include the following. Do you not only determine what the person does, but also control how and when he must do it? Is his work part of your company's business? Does he provide his own equipment and his own assistants? What is his financial interest in his work? Does he receive a fixed salary, sick pay or paid holidays? Is he allowed to work for other companies? No one item is conclusive. If there is doubt in any case, you should consider taking professional advice *before* recruiting your staff or contracting for self-employed staff.

(ii)   Are there any rules on how staff can be recruited?

Yes, many.

Recruitment advertising

Advertisements must not show any intention to discriminate unlawfully by sex. There is a similar prohibition against discrimination by race. However, where sex or race is a genuine occupational qualification for a job, discrimination may be acceptable. In general, you cannot use job descriptions with a particular sexual or racial connotation. For example, 'sales girl' is unacceptable – use 'sales assistant'.

Interviewing and selection

You are not allowed to discriminate by sex or race in your arrangements for deciding who should be offered an interview. Furthermore, you are not allowed to require information to be given on an application form or to ask questions at an interview in respect of certain past criminal convictions where the offender has been rehabilitated and is entitled to treat the conviction as spent.

Offers of employment

You are not allowed to discriminate by sex or race either by refusing or deliberately omitting to offer a person employment or in the terms of employment that you offer a person.

Disability discrimination

Since December 1996, when the Disability Discrimination Act 1995 came into force, employers have been required to treat disabled persons no less favourably than other persons, unless there are justifiable reasons. Consequently, they are not permitted to discriminate against disabled people in advertisements, in the arrangements they make to interview applicants for a job, in the terms of their employment or by refusing or omitting to offer them employment. Employers also have to make reasonable adjustments to the workplace to accommodate disabled employees. These provisions do not apply to employers with less than 20 employees.

Further, if your company employs, on average, more than 250 employees in the UK each week during its financial year, the Directors' Report attached to the company's annual financial statements must contain a statement that describes the company's policy during the year in respect of the following:

■ For giving full and fair consideration (having regard to the person's particular aptitudes and abilities) to applications for employment from disabled persons.

■ For continuing the employment of, and arranging the appropriate training for, any of the company's employees who have become disabled during the period in which the company employed them.

■ Otherwise for the training, the career development and the promotion of those disabled persons the company employs.

(iii) What are the formalities involved in employing a person?

References

When you make an offer of employment it is usual to make the offer 'subject to references satisfactory to us being obtained'. This provides you with some assurance that the person actually has the experience he claims and may also provide you with other valuable information as to whether he will be a good employee. Frequently, employers make use of a standard form of reference enquiry to ensure that the matters they are concerned with are covered.

There are two further advantages to this process. First, you may be required to take up references under the terms of fidelity insurance if your employees regularly handle cash as part of their work. Secondly, you may be able to sue a person who gives a reference negligently.

When giving a reference, an employer has a duty to take reasonable care in its preparation. Indeed, he may be liable to the employee in negligence if he fails to do so and the employee thereby suffers damage.

Documentary evidence of the right to work in the UK

Employers must ensure before they employ a person that he or she has the right to be employed in the UK. This is dealt with in paragraph (xiii) below.

The contract of employment

There is no more need in law for a contract of employment to be in writing than any other type of general contract. You are, however, under a legal duty to give your employees a written statement of certain specific particulars of employment no later than two months after the beginning of employment. The main particulars to be given include:

■ The names of the employer and the employee.

■ The date when the employment began.

■ The date on which the employee's period of 'continuous' employment began. This should take into account any employment with a previous employer which in law must count towards that period, such as employment with an associated company immediately preceding.

■ The scale, rate or method of calculating pay. The requirement as to a minimum wage will need to be taken into account when regulations under the National Minimum Wage Act 1998 comes into force.

■ The intervals at which the employee will be paid.

■ Any terms and conditions relating to working hours. The Working Time Regulations 1998 now restrict an employer's ability to make his employees work long hours. It may, for instance, prevent your employees working for more than 48 hours per week on average (calculated over a 17 week period). This is unless you have their written agreement to work more than this and comply with certain other requirements, such as, to maintain up-to-date records of hours worked by those employees. See also paragraph (x) below.

- Any terms and conditions relating any to the following: holiday entitlement, incapacity for work due to sickness or injury, including sick pay; and pensions and pension schemes.

- The length of notice to which the employee is entitled and must give to terminate his employment, or the date of termination, where it is fixed.

- The place of work.

- The job title and description.

- Whether a 'contracting-out certificate' for pension purposes in force.

- Disciplinary rules and procedures, unless you employ less than 20 employees.

- The person to whom the employee can go if he has a grievance.

- Whether there are any collective agreements with trade unions affecting the employment.

The fact that these particulars are required does not mean that you must provide for them in your agreement with an employee. If there is no such term, all you need do is to state that fact in the written statement.

A written statement need not necessarily constitute a contract of employment. However, a contract constitutes an opportunity to state clearly any additional terms and conditions of employment applicable to the employment relationship. As many of these may protect the employer, it is good practice to have properly drafted contracts for employees that go beyond the minimum requirements of the written statement. However, you should be aware that, in a given situation, the written contract you have with an employee may not represent all of the terms of his contract of employment. Other terms and conditions may become part of the contract: some will be implied by law and others may have been created through custom and practice. Sometimes terms are incorporated into the contract from other documents, such as, collective agreements.

Itemised pay statements

All employers must give their employees a written pay statement before or when wages or salary are paid. This must itemise:

- The gross amount of the wages or salary.
- The amount of any deductions and why they are made.
- The net amount of wages or salary payable.
- Where the net amount is paid in different ways, the amount and method of each.

Pay As You Earn (PAYE)

Where an employee receives salary which is taxable, his employer is responsible for deducting income tax and national insurance contributions from his salary under the PAYE system. The Inland Revenue enforces the operation of the PAYE system strictly and investigates suspected breaches. You must ensure that your company complies with the relevant legislation. Full treatment of this important subject is outside the scope of this book. Detailed instructions on the operation of PAYE are contained in the Inland Revenue booklet *Employer's Guide to PAYE* obtainable from the local tax office.

Employers' liability insurance

All employers who carry on business in Great Britain must take out an 'approved' insurance policy with an 'authorised' insurer against liability for injury or disease sustained by their employees arising out of and in the course of their employment in Great Britain in that business. A copy of the certificate of insurance must be displayed at every place where the employer carries on business so that it can be easily seen and read by all employees. Since 1995 employers' liability insurance may be taken out by a holding company to cover itself and its group.

(iv)   Can my company pay its employees by cheque or must it pay by cash?

It used to be the case that employers had to pay manual workers in cash, unless the person consented to payment by cheque. The method of payment is now a matter to be decided by you and your employee in agreeing upon the terms of the contract of employment.

(v)   Can my company make any deductions from employees' wages?

Yes, but only in certain situations, for example:

- The deduction is required or permitted under a statutory provision, for example, an attachment of earnings order, PAYE or NI.

- The deduction is required or permitted under the employee's contract of employment.

- The employee has given his prior written consent.

- The employee is in *retail* employment, in which case you are entitled to deduct up to one-tenth of the gross wages to the employee for a particular pay-day in respect of cash shortages or stock deficiencies. However, you must have obtained the employee's prior agreement to such deductions and follow strict rules.

(vi)   Do I have to provide pensions and life assurance for my employees?

No. You are not obliged to make any provision for pensions or life assurance. However, many employers do provide a pension benefit for staff, either by offering membership of an occupational pension scheme or by making contributions to the employee's personal pension plan.

Employees who fulfil the necessary requirements, for instance, by their contribution record, may, on retirement, receive a State pension. This is made up of two main components; a basic flat rate pension and an additional earnings related pension (SERPS). However, employees can now have their contributions to the SERPS component replaced by a pension from their employer's occupational pension scheme or through a personal pension plan. In this case employees will not be entitled to the earnings related component of the state pension.

Occupational pension schemes have become more and more important as a benefit to staff. There are also tax benefits for employers who set up pension and life assurance schemes, making such arrangements a tax efficient method of remuneration. You should appreciate, however, that occupational pension schemes, particularly those offering benefits linked to final salary (defined benefit) schemes are increasingly highly regulated and can, therefore, involve substantial administrative cost.

For all but the largest companies, it is important to insure any life assurance benefit, or dependant's pension payable in the event of an employee dying whilst in service to avoid any catastrophic risk. The cost of insurance is relatively inexpensive.

(vii) Do I have to pay my employees if they are ill?

Subject to certain exceptions, you may be liable to pay a sick employee 'statutory sick pay' (SSP). The most important exceptions from this obligation are where the employee's average weekly earnings are below the lower earnings limit for National Insurance contribution purposes, or where the employee's contract of service was entered into for a specified period of not more than three calendar months. A series of contracts taking effect consecutively will be treated as one contract when calculating whether the period of three months has been exceeded.

You must, therefore, pay a qualifying employee SSP if he has been sick for at least four consecutive days (including Sundays and Public Holidays) during which he was too ill to work, has notified you of this and supplied evidence of the sickness. The maximum entitlement to SSP over a three-year period is generally 28 weeks, after which an employee must claim state incapacity benefit. There are fixed rates of SSP payable. Detailed records relating to SSP must be kept for three years.

If you do not make this payment, the employee is entitled to require written reasons for your decision, against which he can appeal before a local social security tribunal.

Apart from the obligation to pay SSP, your obligation to pay an employee during periods of sickness depend upon his contract of employment. Many employers in the UK specifically provide that payment over and above SSP is at the employer's discretion.

You will find the DSS booklet *Employers' Manual on Statutory Sick Pay* CA 30 helpful in administering SSP. This is available from the Contributions Agency.

(viii) What happens if an employee becomes pregnant?

Maternity rights in the UK are complex. Set out here is the very briefest of summaries. All women employees are now entitled to take a period of maternity absence of 14 weeks. This right is not dependent on hours worked or length of service. Women with two years' service have additional rights, essentially permitting a longer period of maternity leave.

You cannot dismiss an employee for a reason connected with her pregnancy without the dismissal being automatically unfair or, potentially, sexual discrimination (see paragraph (xv) of this appendix). A pregnant woman also has the right to take paid time off for antenatal care and to return to work after her confinement.

A pregnant employee may also qualify for 'statutory maternity pay' (SMP) for 18 consecutive weeks beginning no earlier than the 11th week before the expected week of childbirth.

You will find the SS booklet *Employers' Manual on Statutory Maternity Pay* CA 29 helpful in administering SMP. This is also available from the Contributions Agency.

(ix)   Are my employees entitled to holiday or holiday pay?

Historically, this has depended entirely on your contract of employment with your employee and most employers do grant an annual holiday entitlement to their staff. However, from 1 October 1998, this is mandatory under the Working Time Regulations 1998. These Regulations entitle employees (and many self-employed staff) to three weeks' paid holiday, rising to four weeks each year from November 1999. Other aspects of the Regulations are dealt with in paragraph (x) below.

(x)   What are my responsibilities for my employees' health and safety at work?

This is a very complicated subject as, in addition to the general common law and statutory duties relating to safety imposed on employers, there are special regulations governing particular industries and particularly hazardous occupations. The following should, therefore, be considered only an outline of your responsibilities in this area.

Over the years the courts have established wide-ranging duties on employers to take care of their employees, which stem from basic safety rules, one of which is that an employer must take reasonable care not to subject his employees to unnecessary risk. If you are negligent in performing these duties you may be liable to a claim for damages by your employees (although you are bound to insure against this liability anyway – see paragraph (iii) above).

Employers' statutory duties

Some of employers' more important general statutory duties relating to health and safety at work are summarised below.

General duties of employers to their employees – The general common law duties mentioned above are restated in very similar terms in the Health and Safety at Work Act 1974 which imposes on employers criminal liability for breach of the legislation. However, if your company fails to comply with the legislation, you, personally, may also be guilty of an offence (see below).

Section 2 of the 1974 Act contains the following general statement of employers' responsibilities:

> *"It shall be the duty of every employer to ensure, so far as is reasonably practicable, the health, safety and welfare at work of all his employees".*

This duty is then specifically stated to include matters relating to: plant; systems of work; handling, transport and storage of goods; health and safety training and supervision of employees; and the working environment and work place. In addition, companies must publish a safety policy and consult safety representatives.

Safety policies – As an employer, you are required, if you employ five or more employees, to prepare and keep up to date a written statement of your general policy regarding health and safety at work and the organisation and arrangements for carrying out that policy. This must be brought to the attention of all employees and be placed in an accessible position.

Safety representatives – Where the employer recognises a trade union, that union has the right to appoint representatives to represent the employees in consultations with employers regarding arrangements for promoting and developing measures to ensure the health and safety at work of the employees and checking their effectiveness. They may request their employer to set up a *safety committee* to review these arrangements. They may also be involved in investigating potential hazards and complaints. In certain circumstances you must give facilities and allow time off for the training of the representatives. Where no trade union is recognised employers are now required by the Health and Safety (Consultation with Employees) Regulations 1996 to consult their employees about health and safety matters either directly or through representatives elected by the employees.

Record keeping – A feature of the legislation that is of practical daily importance to you is the need to maintain an 'accident book'. All employers must keep records of any deaths, major injuries and dangerous occurrences at work. They must also keep records of certain diseases. These 'reportable' diseases are generally occupational ones.

In addition, employers are under a duty to report such deaths, injuries, and dangerous occurrences as quickly as possible to the relevant authority. This notification must be followed by a report in writing to the relevant authority within ten days on the prescribed form. Where a reportable disease has been confirmed by a medical practitioner, the employer must immediately send a report on the prescribed to the relevant authority. The relevant authority will usually be your local authority or may be the Health and Safety Executive.

The Health and Safety at Work Act 1974 is supplemented in key areas by a series of health and safety Regulations. These areas include the following: management of health and safety at work; display screen equipment; personal protective equipment at work; provision and use of work equipment; manual handling operations; workplace requirements dealing with health, safety and welfare. The Health and Safety Executive has published guidance notes on these subjects.

General enquiries and guidance on publications regarding health and safety legislation may be made by telephone to the Health and Safety Executive (HSE) Infoline on 0541 545500. A catalogue of HSE publications can be obtained from HSE Books, PO Box 1999, Sudbury, Suffolk CO10 6FS,. Tel: 01787 881165 Fax 01787 313995. Information about new publications can also be obtained from the HSE site on the World Wide Web http://www.open.gov.uk/hse/hsehome.htm

Enforcement of the health and safety legislation

Enforcement is by inspectors of the Health and Safety Executive or, where it is not the enforcing authority, the local authority. Inspectors have the right to enter and inspect premises and bring prosecutions for unsafe practices. They can also issue improvement notices requiring an employer to remedy specific problems and prohibition notices. Prohibition notices require activities that the inspector considers involve risk of serious personal injury to be stopped, unless the matters specified are remedied.

Breaches of the legislation can lead to criminal proceedings. The main offences, for instance, breach of the employer's duty to his employees under section 2 of the Health and Safety at Work Act 1974 or for refusing to comply with an improvement or prohibition notice carries a maximum fine of

£20,000 and/or imprisonment for up to six months if the proceedings are in the magistrates court. If proceedings are taken in the Crown Court, the penalty can be an unlimited fine and/or up to two years imprisonment. Imprisonment will generally only be imposed where there has been gross negligence or neglect.

A director or manager of the employing company will also be liable if it is proved that the offence has been committed by the company with his consent or connivance or that it is attributable to his neglect. In addition, a director who is found guilty may also be disqualified under section 2 of the Company Directors Disqualification Act 1986– on conviction of an indictable offence (see question 13.3 above) – as it has been held to extend to health and safety matters.

The Working Time Regulations 1998

These Regulations, effective from 1 October 1998, impose certain obligations on employers. They are enforceable by the Health and Safety Executive and local authorities and by employees themselves. These obligations include the following matters. The maximum average weekly working time of workers is not to exceed 48 hours (calculated over a 17 week period) without the individual worker's written agreement. The average normal hours of night workers is not to exceed eight for each 24 hours and night workers are entitled to be given free health assessment at regular intervals. Employers must keep records of workers' hours of work. Workers must be given rest breaks where the daily working time is more than six hours and daily and weekly rest periods of a specified length.

(xi)   What if my employees belong to a trade union?

Currently in the UK you have no obligation to recognise a trade union in respect of your work force although the Government has well publicised plans to give unions a right of recognition in certain circumstances.

Where you do recognise a trade union for the purposes of collective bargaining you owe certain obligations to the union. The most important are:

- The trade union is entitled to certain collective bargaining information as of right.

- The trade union can demand to be consulted on pending redundancies.

- The trade union can demand to be consulted on a planned transfer of the employer's undertaking.

- The trade union is entitled to appoint safety representatives (see above).

In addition, individual employees who are members of the trade union will have certain rights that they can enforce against you. The most important are:

- Where an employee is a trade union official, he is entitled to take reasonable time off during his working hours to carry out his duties and undergo training and be paid during the time off.

- Where an employee is a trade union member, he is entitled to reasonable time off during his working hours to take part in certain trade union activities (not extending to industrial action) although he is not entitled to be paid during the time off.

These rights apply only where the trade union is 'independent', a requirement basically that the trade union is not under the control of the employer. A trade union that is independent will invariably have a certificate from the Certification Officer of Trade Unions to prove this.

In addition, an employee has a right not to have detrimental action taken against him or to be dismissed for membership of, or taking part in, the activities of a trade union. Where an employee is dismissed for this reason the dismissal is automatically unfair.

(xii)   How does the discrimination legislation affect my company?

In general terms, you must not discriminate against an employee on the grounds of disability, race or sex in the way that you offer that employee access to opportunities for promotion, transfer or training. This also includes refusing access to any other benefits, facilities or services or by refusing or deliberately omitting to afford him or her access to them or in the terms of employment afforded him or her. Nor can you subject an employee to any other detriment on the grounds of disability, race or sex. Sexual harassment is a specific example of this, and you can, as employer, find yourself liable for the actions one of your staff may inflict on another. The need for awareness of these issues and to educate staff on how to treat and respect colleagues is growing in importance. Discrimination is an increasingly difficult, and potentially damaging, area of UK employment law. If you face allegations of discrimination, for instance, in the area of sexual harassment, you would be wise to take appropriate professional advice.

(xiii)   Can I take on foreign employees?

The Asylum and Immigration Act 1996 imposes onerous duties on employers as, from January 1997, it has been a criminal offence to offer a job to a person who does not have the right to take employment in the UK, because he is subject to immigration controls.

To avoid committing an offence, employers now need to check, before employment begins, that the employee has one of a wide range of documents that give the right to work in the UK; for instance, a document issued by a previous employer giving their National Insurance number; a passport describing the holder as a British citizen; a birth certificate issued in the UK, the Republic of Ireland, the Channel Islands or the Isle of Man; a passport or national identity card issued by a Member State of the European Economic Area (EEA) describing the person as a national of that State; a work permit issued by the Department of Education and Employment; or a passport or other document endorsed to show that the holder has leave to enter the UK and is not precluded from taking the employment in question.

The Act does not, however, apply to employment which began before 27 January 1997. The EEA consists of the 15 member states of the European Community plus Iceland, Liechtenstein and Norway. At the time of writing the following are members of the EC: Austria, Belgium, Denmark, Eire, Finland, France, Germany, Greece, Holland, Italy, Luxembourg, Portugal, Spain, Sweden and the United Kingdom.

(xiv)   How do I dismiss a person?

You can give the person the notice they are entitled to or, if they are guilty of gross misconduct (for example, theft), you can dismiss an employee 'summarily', that is, without notice.

If you dismiss without giving notice when you are not entitled to do so, you will be acting in breach of the contract of employment. This will result in the dismissal being 'wrongful' and the employee may be entitled to damages for breach of contract. The employee is entitled (unless he is guilty of gross misconduct) to a minimum period of notice by statute, which depends upon his length of service, although the contract of employment may specify a longer period. In addition, a longer notice period may be implied into a contract of employment if this is reasonable in the circumstances.

What you also need to be concerned with is that you do not dismiss an employee unfairly (see paragraph (xv) below). Employees have a right not to be unfairly dismissed even if you give the correct period of notice. If an Industrial Tribunal decides that your dismissal was unfair, it could order that the employee be reinstated or be paid compensation.

How much notice must I give an employee?

Statute lays down minimum periods of notice that an employee is entitled to receive. After one month's continuous employment the employee must be given at least one week's notice. This rises to two weeks after two years continuous service and then an additional week for each additional year of service subject to a maximum of 12 weeks (after 12 years of service). The contract of employment may provide for a longer period. If the contract is silent on the question of notice, the period given must be 'reasonable' which could, in certain circumstances, be longer than the statutory minimum.

What form of 'notice' is necessary?

The actual form of the notice will depend upon what is required in the contract of employment. Usually, any clear written notice will suffice for that purpose. However, the law provides that an employee is entitled to be given a written statement giving details of the reasons for his dismissal if he has been employed for more than two years, or if she is pregnant or on maternity leave.

(xv) When is a dismissal 'unfair'?

To bring a claim for unfair dismissal an employee must first of all show that he has been employed for the requisite qualifying period and has been *dismissed.* The statutory qualifying period is currently two years, but this is being challenged as being discriminatory against women, which could mean the qualification period is only one year. If the reason for the dismissal is discrimination, trade union membership, health and safety matters or pregnancy this qualifying period does not apply.

To determine whether the dismissal was fair or unfair, you, as the employer, will have to show that the principal ground for the dismissal was one of five grounds justifying dismissal. These are:

- That it related to the capability of the employee for performing his work.

- That it related to the employee's conduct, for example, violence at work.

- That the employee was redundant.

- That the employee could not have continued to work in that position without breaking the law in some way.

- That it was for some other substantial reason of a kind such as to justify the dismissal.

There are some grounds for dismissal that can never be acceptable including:

- Where the dismissal is 'union-related', for example, because the employee took part in trade union activities.

- Where the dismissal is on the grounds of pregnancy.

- Where the dismissal was related to health and safety issues.

- Where the reason for the dismissal relates to an employee's action to secure certain other statutory rights, such as the right to a minimum wage or the right to holiday entitlement.

- Where the dismissal took place in connection with the transfer of an undertaking. However, a dismissal for economic, technical or organisational reasons entailing a change in the work force can be fair.

Even if you can show that there was an acceptable ground for dismissing an employee, an Industrial Tribunal will still have to decide whether the dismissal was, in all the circumstances, fair or unfair. This is a test of whether the procedure followed was fair and the employer acted reasonably in carrying out the dismissal.

For an employee to claim that he has been unfairly dismissed, he must present his claim to an Industrial Tribunal within three months of the date of the termination of the employment, or some other period considered reasonable where it is not practical to comply with that time limit.

Table of requirements for a company's statutory books

Register or book	Companies Act 1985 reference	Where to be kept	Whether available for public inspection
Register of Interests in Shares (public companies only)	S.211	With Register of Directors' Interests in Shares and Debentures	Yes
Register of Directors and Secretaries	S.288 to 290	At Registered Office	Yes
Register of Directors' Interests in Shares and Debentures	S.325	At Registered Office or with Register of members	Yes
Register of Members	S.352 to 353	At Registered office or some other place (if within the country in which the company is registered and if notified to the Registrar of Companies)	Yes
Minutes of shareholders', directors' and managers' meetings	S.382 to 383	At Registered Office (shareholders' meetings)	No, but shareholders may inspect minutes of shareholders meetings
		Where directors decide (directors' and managers' meetings)	No
Register of Charges	S.407	At Registered Office	Yes

Directors' service contracts	S.318	At Registered Office, with the Register of Members or the company's principle place of business (if within the country in which the company is registered)	No, but shareholders may inspect
Accounting records	S.221 to 222	At the Registered Office or where directors decide	No

Section 214 of the Insolvency Act 1986 (wrongful trading)

214 – Wrongful Trading

(1)   Subject to subsection (3) below, if in the course of the winding-up of a company it appears that subsection (2) of this section applies in relation to a person who is or has been a director of the company, the court, on the application of the liquidator, may declare that that person is to be liable to make such contribution (if any) to the company's assets as the court thinks proper.

(2)   This subsection applies in relation to a person if:

(a)   the company has gone into insolvent liquidation,

(b)   at some time before the commencement of the winding up of the company, that person knew or ought to have concluded that there was no reasonable prospect that the company would avoid going into insolvent liquidation, and

(c)   that person was a director of the company at that time;

but the court shall not make a declaration under this section in any case where the time mentioned in paragraph (b) above was before 28 April 1986.

(3)   The court shall not make a declaration under this Section with respect to any person if it is satisfied that after the condition specified in subsection (2)(b) was first satisfied in relation to him that person took every step with a view to minimising the potential loss to the company's creditors as (assuming him to have known that there was no reasonable prospect that

the company would avoid going into insolvent liquidation) he ought to have taken.

(4)   For the purposes of subsections (2) and (3), the facts which a director of a company ought to know or ascertain, the conclusions which he ought to reach and the steps which he ought to take are those which would be known or ascertained, or reached or taken, by a reasonably diligent person having both:

(a)   the general knowledge, skill and experience that may reasonably be expected of a person carrying out the same functions as are carried out by that director in relation to the company, and

(b)   the general knowledge, skill and experience that that director has.

(5)   The reference in subsection (4) to the functions carried out in relation to a company by a director of the company includes any functions which he does not carry out but which have been entrusted to him.

(6)   For the purposes of this section a company goes into insolvent liquidation if it goes into liquidation at a time when its assets are insufficient for the payment of its debts and other liabilities and the expenses of the winding up.

(7)   In this section 'director' includes a shadow director.

(8)   This section is without prejudice to section 213.

Table of criminal offences of which directors and other officers may be convicted

The table below summarises only the criminal offences contained in the Companies Act 1985 of which both directors and other officers may be convicted. There are, however, many other offences that a company may have to face that have consequences for directors and other officers. A full list of offences under the Companies Act 1985 is contained in Schedule 24 of that Act. Of course, directors and other officers may also be liable for criminal offences committed under other Acts of Parliament and these are not dealt with here. The fines given reflect the new levels effective from 1.10.92

The Companies Act 1985

Section of Act creating offence	General nature of offence	Mode of prosecution	Punishment	Daily default fine (where applicable)
80(9)	Directors exercising company's power or allotment without the authority required by section 80(1)	1. On indictment 2. Summary	Unlimited fine £5,000	
88(5)	Officer of company failing to deliver return of allotments etc, to Registrar	1. On indictment 2. Summary	Unlimited fine £5,000	£500
95(6)	Knowingly or recklessly authorising or permitting misleading, false or deceptive material in statement by directors under section 95(5)	1. On indictment 2. Summary	2 years or unlimited fine, or both 6 months or £5,000 or both	

111(3)	Officer of company failing to deliver copy of asset valuation report to Registrar	1. On indictment 2. Summary	Unlimited fine £5,000	£500
141	Officer of company concealing name of creditor entitled to object to reduction of capital, or wilfully misrepresenting nature or amount of debt or claim, etc.	1. On indictment 2. Summary	Unlimited fine. £5,000 fine.	
142(2)	Director authorising or permitting non-compliance with section 142 (requirement to convene company meeting to consider serious loss of capital)	1. On indictment 2. Summary	Unlimited fine. £5,000 fine.	
156(7)	Director making statutory declaration under section 155, without having reasonable grounds	1. On indictment 2. Summary	2 years or unlimited fine, or both. 6 months or £5,000 or both.	
169(6)	Default by company's officer in delivery to Registrar of the return required by section 169.	1. On indictment 2. Summary	Unlimited fine. £5,000.	£500
173(6)	Director making statutory declaration under section 173 without having reasonable grounds for the opinion expressed in the declaration.	1. On indictment 2. Summary	2 years or unlimited fine, or both. 6 months or £5,000 or both.	
221(5) or 222(4)	Company failing to keep accounting records (liability of officers).	1. On indictment 2. Summary	2 years or unlimited fine, or both. 6 months or £5,000 or both.	

222(6)	Officer of company failing to secure compliance with, or internationally causing default under, section 222(5) (preservation of accounting records for requisite number of years).	1. On indictment 2. Summary	2 years or unlimited fine, or both 6 months or £5,000 or both.
232(4)	Default by director or officer of a company in giving notice of matters relating to himself for purposes of Schedule 6 Part I.	Summary	£1,000 fine.
233(5)	Approving defective accounts.	1. On indictment 2. Summary	Unlimited fine. £5,000 fine.
233(6)	Laying or delivery of unsigned balance sheet; circulating copies of balance sheet without signatures.	Summary	£1,000.
234(5)	Non-compliance with Part VII, as to directors' report and its content; directors individually liable.	1. On indictment 2. Summary	Unlimited fine. £5,000.
234A(4)	Laying, circulating or delivering directors' report without required signature.	Summary	£1,000 fine
236(4)	Laying, circulating or delivering auditors' report without required signature	Summary	£1,000 fine.
238(5)	Failing to send company's annual accounts, directors' report and auditors' report to those entitled to receive them.	1. On indictment 2. Summary	Unlimited fine. £5,000 fine.
240(6)	Failure to comply with requirements in connection with publication of accounts.	Summary	£1,000 fine.

241(2) or 242(2)	Director in default as regards duty to lay and deliver company's annual accounts, directors' report and auditors' report.	Summary	£5,000 fine.	£500
251(6)	Failure to comply with requirements in relation to summary financial statements.	Summary	£1,000 fine.	
288(4)	Default in complying with section 288 (keeping register of directors and secretaries, refusal of inspection).	Summary	£5,000 fine.	£500
291(5)	Acting as director of a company without having the requisite share qualification.	Summary	£1,000 fine.	£100
294(3)	Director failing to give notice of his attaining retirement age; acting as director under appointment invalid due to his attaining it.	Summary	£1,000 fine.	£100
305(3)	Company default in complying with section 305 (directors' names on company correspondence, etc).	Summary	£1,000 fine.	
306(4)	Failure to state that liability of proposed director or manager is unlimited; failure to give notice of that fact to person accepting office.	1. On indictment 2. Summary	Unlimited fine. £5,000 fine.	
314(3)	Director failing to comply with section 314 (duty to disclose compensation payable on takeover, etc); a person's failure to include required particulars in a notice he has to give of such matters.	Summary	£1,000 fine.	

317(7)	Director failing to disclose interest in contract.	1. On indictment 2. Summary	Unlimited fine. £5,000 fine.	
318(8)	Company default in complying with section 318(1) or (5) (directors' service contracts to be open to inspection); 14 days' default in complying with section 318(4) (notice to Registrar as to where copies of contracts and memoranda are kept); refusal of inspection required under section 318(7).	Summary	£1,000 fine.	£100
322B (4)	Terms of unwritten contract between sole members of a private company limited by shares or by guarantee and the company not set out on a written memorandum or recorded in minutes of directors' meeting	Summary	£5,000 fine.	
323(2)	Director dealing in options to buy or sell company's listed shares or debentures.	1. On indictment 2. Summary	2 years or unlimited fine, or both. 6 months or £5,000 or both.	
324(7)	Director failing to notify interest in company's shares; making false statement in purported notification.	1. On indictment 2. Summary	2 years or unlimited fine, or both. 6 months or £5,000 or both.	
326(2), (3), (4), (5)	Various defaults in connection with company register of directors' interests.	Summary	£1000 fine.	Except in the case of section 326(5), £100.

328(6)	Director failing to notify company that members of his family have, or have exercised, options to buy shares or debentures; making false statement in purported notification.	1. On indictment 2. Summary	2 years or unlimited fine, or both. 6 months or £5,000 or both.	
329(3)	Company failing to notify investment exchange of acquisition of its securities by a director.	Summary	£1,000 fine.	£100.
342(2)	Relevant company entering into transaction or arrangement for a director in contravention of section 330.	1. On indictment 2. Summary	2 years or unlimited fine, or both. 6 months or £5,000 or both.	
342(3)	Procuring a relevant company to enter into transaction or arrangement known to be contrary to section 330.	1. On indictment 2. Summary	2 years or unlimited fine, or both. 6 months or £5,000 or both.	
343(8)	Company failing to maintain register of transactions, etc, made with and for directors and not disclosed in company accounts; failing to make register available at Registered Office or at company meeting.	1. On indictment 2. Summary	Unlimited fine. £5,000.	
349(3)	Officer of company issuing business letter or document not bearing company's name	Summary	£1,000 fine.	
349(4)	Officer of company signing cheque, bill of exchange, etc, on which company's name not mentioned.	Summary	£1,000 fine.	
350(2)	Officer of company, etc, using company seal without name engraved on it.	Summary	£1,000 fine.	

351(5)(b)	Officer or agent of company issuing, or authorising issue of, business document not complying with those subsections.	Summary	£1,000 fine.	
381B(2)	Director or secretary of company failing to notify auditors of proposed written resolution.	Summary	£1,000 fine.	
392A(5)	Directors failing to convene meeting requestioned by resigning auditor	1. On indictment 2. Summary	Unlimited fine. £5,000 fine.	
408(3)	Officer of company refusing inspection of charging instrument or register of charges.	Summary	£1,000 fine.	£100
426(7)	Director or trustee for debenture holders failing to give notice to company of matters necessary for purposes of section 426.	Summary	£1,000 fine.	
450	Destroying or mutilating company documents falsifying such documents or making false entries parting with such documents or altering them or making omissions.	1. On indictment 2. Summary	7 years or unlimited fine, or both. 6 months or £5,000, or both.	
451	Making false statement or explanation in purported compliance with section 447.	1. On indictment 2. Summary	2 years or unlimited fine, or both. 6 months or £5,000, or both.	
458	Being a party to carrying on company's business with intent to defraud creditors, or for any fraudulent purpose.	1. On indictment 2. Summary	7 years or unlimited fine, or both. 6 months or £5,000 or both.	

Appendix VI

Directors' loans decision tables

Decision table 1: Loans – relevant company

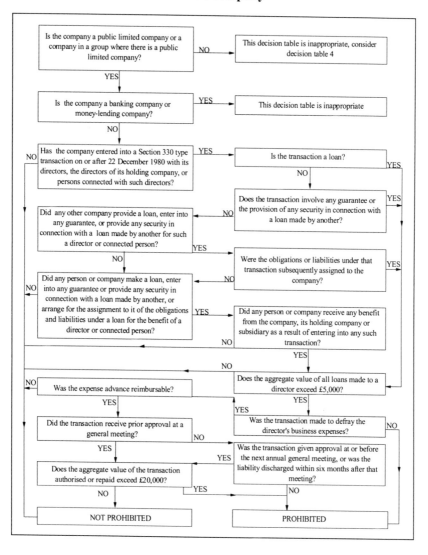

253

Decision table 2: Quasi-loans – relevant company

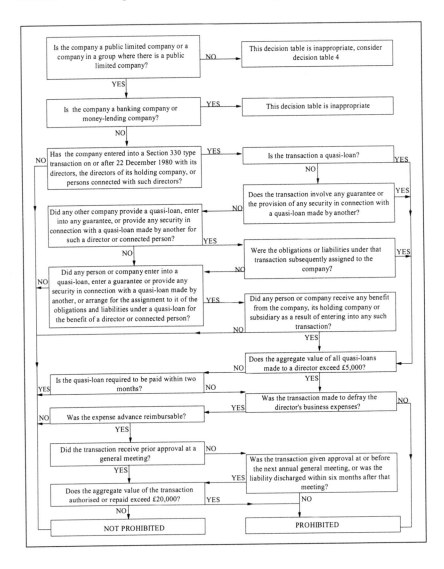

Decision table 3: Credit transactions – relevant company

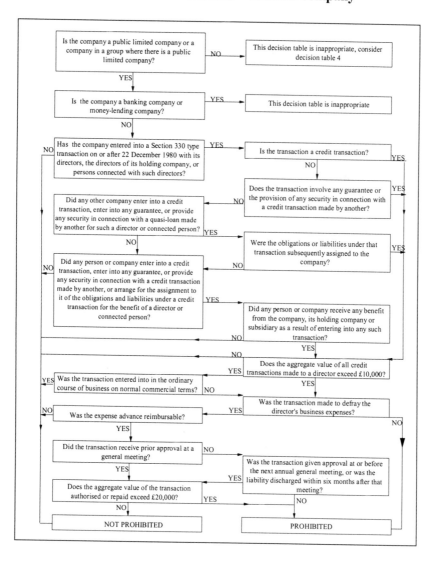

Decision table 4: Loans – non-relevant company

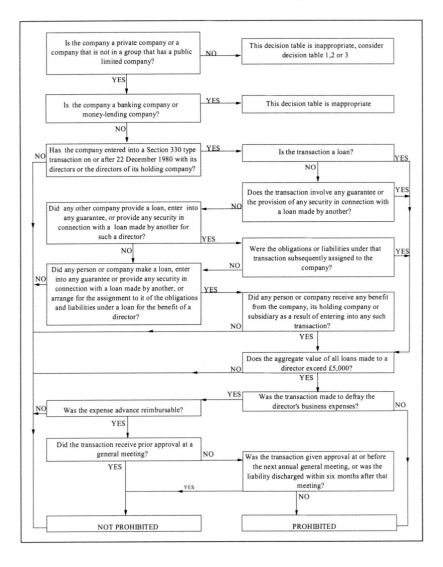

The Combined Code

Reproduced below is the full text of the Combined Code issued by the Committee on Corporate Governance in June 1998.

Principles of good governance and code of best practice

Derived by the Committee on Corporate Governance from the Committee's Final Report and from the Cadbury and Greenbury Reports.

Preamble

1   In the Committee's final report we said that, in response to many requests, we intended to produce a set of principles and code which embraced Cadbury, Greenbury and the Committee's own work. This Combined Code fulfils that undertaking.

2   The Combined Code is now issued in final form, and includes a number of changes made by The London Stock Exchange, with the Committee's agreement, following the consultation undertaken by the Exchange on the Committee's original draft.

3   The Combined Code contains both principles and detailed code provisions. We understand that it is the intention of the London Stock Exchange to introduce a requirement on listed companies to make a disclosure statement in two parts.

4   In the first part of the statement, the company will be required to report on how it applies the principles in the Combined Code. We make clear in our report that we do not prescribe the form or content of this part of the statement, the intention being that companies should have a free hand to explain their governance policies in the light of the principles, including any special circumstances applying to them which have led to a particular

approach. It must be for shareholders and others to evaluate this part of the company's statement.

5   In the second part of the statement the company will he required either to confirm that it complies with the Code provisions or – where it does not – provide an explanation. Again, it must be for shareholders and others to evaluate such explanations.

6   In our report we make clear that companies should be ready to explain their governance policies, including any circumstances justifying departure from best practice; and that those concerned with the evaluation of governance should do so with common sense and with due regard to companies' individual circumstances.

7   We also make clear in our report that it is still too soon to assess definitively the results of the Cadbury and, more especially, the Greenbury codes. We see this Combined Code as a consolidation of the work of the three committees, not as a new departure. We have therefore retained the substance of the two earlier codes except in those few cases where we take a different view from our predecessors. We should in particular like to make clear, in relation to the detailed provisions in the Listing Rules on directors' remuneration, that we envisage no change except where we take a different view from the Greenbury committee. With two exceptions, relating to the status of the remuneration committee, and the compensation payable to an executive director on loss of office, these changes are minor.

8   Section 1 of the Combined Code contains the corporate governance principles and code provisions applicable to all listed companies incorporated in the United Kingdom. These would be covered by the statement referred to in paragraphs 3–5 above, which will be required by the Listing Rules. Section 2 contains principles and code provisions applicable to institutional shareholders with regard to their voting, dialogue with companies and evaluation of a company's governance arrangements. These are not matters which are appropriate for the Listing Rules to include within the disclosure requirement. Nevertheless we regard Section 2 of the Combined Code as an integral part of our recommendations; we commend it to the organisations

representing institutional shareholders and we hope that at least the major institutions will voluntarily disclose to their clients and the public the extent to which they are able to give effect to these provisions.

9   We have not included in the Combined Code principle D.IV in Chapter 2 of our final report, which reads as follows:

"External Auditors. The external auditors should independently report to shareholders in accordance with statutory and professional requirements and independently assure the board on the discharge of its responsibilities under D.I and D.II above in accordance with professional guidance."

We say in paragraph 6.7 of the report that we recommend neither any additional prescribed requirements nor the removal of any existing requirements for auditors in relation to governance or publicly reported information, some of which derive from the Listing Rules. This recommendation is accepted by the London Stock Exchange. But the existing requirements for auditors will be kept under review, as a matter of course, by the responsible organisations.

COMMITTEE ON CORPORATE GOVERNANCE
June 1998

The Combined Code

Part 1 – Principles of good governance

Section 1 Companies

A   Directors

The board

1.   Every listed company should be headed by an effective board which should lead and control the company.

Chairman and CEO

2.   There are two key tasks at the top of every public company – the running of the board and the executive responsibility for the running of the company's business. There should be a clear division of responsibilities at the head of the company which will ensure a balance of power and authority, such that no one individual has unfettered powers of decision.

Board balance

3.   The board should include a balance of executive and non-executive directors (including independent non-executives) such that no individual or small group of individuals can dominate the board's decision taking.

Supply of information

4.   The board should be supplied in a timely manner with information in a form and of a quality appropriate to enable it to discharge its duties.

Appointments to the board

5.   There should he a formal and transparent procedure for the appointment of new directors to the board.

Re-election

6.   All directors should be required to submit themselves for re-election at regular intervals and at least every three years.

B. Directors' remuneration

The level and make-up of remuneration

1.   Levels of remuneration should be sufficient to attract and retain the directors needed to run the company successfully, but companies should avoid paying more than is necessary for this purpose. A proportion of executive directors' remuneration should be structured so as to link rewards to corporate and individual performance.

Procedure

2.   Companies should establish a formal and transparent procedure for developing policy on executive remuneration and for fixing the remuneration packages of individual directors. No director should be involved in deciding his or her own remuneration.

Disclosure

3.   The company's annual report should contain a statement of remuneration policy and details of the remuneration of each director.

C. Relations with shareholders

Dialogue with institutional shareholders

1. Companies should be ready, where practicable, to enter into a dialogue with institutional shareholders based on the mutual understanding of objectives.

Constructive use of the AGM

2. Boards should use the AGM to communicate with private investors and encourage their participation.

D. Accountability and audit

Financial reporting

1. The board should present a balanced and understandable assessment of the company's position and prospects.

Internal control

2. The board should maintain a sound system of internal control to safeguard shareholders' investment and the company's assets.

Audit committee and auditors

3. The board should establish formal and transparent arrangements for considering how they should apply the financial reporting and internal control principles and for maintaining an appropriate relationship with the company's auditors.

Section 2 Institutional shareholders

E Institutional investors

Shareholder voting

1. Institutional shareholders have a responsibility to make considered use of their votes.

Dialogue with companies

2. Institutional shareholders should be ready, where practicable, to enter into a dialogue with companies based on the mutual understanding of objectives.

Evaluation of governance disclosures

3. When evaluating companies' governance arrangements, particularly those relating to board structure and composition, institutional investors should give due weight to all relevant factors drawn to their attention.

Part 2 Code of best practice

Section 1 Companies

A.   Directors

A.1   The Board

Principle

Every listed company should be headed by an effective board which should lead and control the company.

Code provisions

A.1.1   The board should meet regularly.

A.1.2   The board should have a formal schedule of matters specifically reserved to it for decision.

A.1.3   There should be a procedure agreed by the board for directors in the furtherance of their duties to take independent professional advice if necessary, at the company's expense.

A.1.4   All directors should have access to the advice and services of the company secretary, who is responsible to the board for ensuring that board procedures are followed and that applicable rules and regulations are complied with. Any question of the removal of the company secretary should he a matter for the board as a whole.

A.1.5   All directors should bring an independent judgement to bear on issues of strategy, performance, resources (including key appointments) and standards of conduct.

A.1.6   Every director should receive appropriate training on the first occasion that he or she is appointed to the board of a listed company, and subsequently as necessary.

A.2 Chairman and CEO

Principle

There are two key tasks at the top of every public company – the running of the board and the executive responsibility for the running of the company's business. There should be a clear division of responsibilities at the head of the company which will ensure a balance of power and authority, such that no one individual has unfettered powers of decision.

Code provision

A.2.1   A decision to combine the posts of chairman and chief executive officer in one person should be publicly justified. Whether the posts are held by different people or by the same person, there should be a strong and independent non-executive element on the board, with a recognised senior member other than the chairman to whom concerns can be conveyed. The chairman, chief executive and senior independent director should be identified in the annual report.

A.3 Board Balance

Principle

The board should include a balance of executive and non-executive directors (including independent non-executives) such that no individual or small group of individuals can dominate the board's decision taking.

Code provisions

A.3.1   The board should include non-executive directors of sufficient calibre and number for their views to carry significant weight in the board's decisions. Non-executive directors should comprise not less than one third of the board.

A.3.2   The majority of non-executive directors should be independent of management and free from any business or other relationship which could materially interfere with the exercise of their independent judgement. Non-executive directors considered by the board to be independent in this sense should be identified in the annual report.

A.4 Supply of Information

Principle

The board should he supplied in a timely manner with information in a form and of a quality appropriate to enable it to discharge its duties.

Code provision

A.4.1   Management has an obligation to provide the board with appropriate and timely information, but information volunteered by management is unlikely to be enough in all circumstances and directors should make further enquiries where necessary. The chairman should ensure that all directors are properly briefed on issues arising at board meetings.

A.5 Appointments to the Board

Principle

There should he a formal and transparent procedure for the appointment of new directors to the board.

Code provision

A.5.1   Unless the board is small, a nomination committee should be established to make recommendations to the board on all new board appointments. A majority of the members of this committee should be non-executive directors and the chairman should be either the chairman of the board or a non-executive director. The chairman and members of the nomination committee should be identified in the annual report.

A.6 Re-election

Principle

All directors should be required to submit themselves for re-election at regular intervals and at least every three years.

Code provisions

A.6.1   Non-executive directors should be appointed for specified terms subject to re-election and to Companies Act provisions relating to the removal of a director, and reappointment should not be automatic.

A.6.2   All directors should be subject to election by shareholders at the first opportunity after their appointment, and to re-election thereafter at intervals of no more than three years. The names of directors submitted for election or re-election should be accompanied by sufficient biographical details to enable shareholders to take an informed decision on their election.

B   Directors' remuneration

B.1 The Level and Make-up of Remuneration

Principle

Levels of remuneration should be sufficient to attract and retain the directors needed to run the company successfully, but companies should avoid paying more than is necessary for this purpose. A proportion of executive directors' remuneration should be structured so as to link rewards to corporate and individual performance.

Code provisions

Remuneration policy

B.1.1   The remuneration committee should provide the packages needed to attract, retain and motivate executive directors of the quality required but should avoid paying more than is necessary for this purpose.

B.1.2   Remuneration committees should judge where to position their company relative to other companies. They should be aware what comparable companies are paying and should take account of relative performance. But they should use such comparisons with caution, in view of the risk that they can result in an upward ratchet of remuneration levels with no corresponding improvement in performance.

B.1.3   Remuneration committees should be sensitive to the wider scene, including pay and employment conditions elsewhere in the group, especially when determining annual salary increases.

B.1.4   The performance-related elements of remuneration should form a significant proportion of the total remuneration package of executive directors and should be designed to align their interests with those of shareholders and to give these directors keen incentives to perform at the highest levels.

B.1.5   Executive share options should not be offered at a discount save as permitted by paragraphs 13.30 and 13.31 of the Listing Rules.

B.1.6   In designing schemes of performance-related remuneration, remuneration committees should follow the provisions in Schedule A to this Code.

Service contracts and compensation

B.1.7   There is a strong case for setting notice or contract periods at, or reducing them to, one year or less. Boards should set this as an objective, but they should recognise that it may not he possible to achieve it immediately.

B.1.8   If it is necessary to offer longer notice or contract periods to new directors recruited from outside, such periods should reduce after the initial period.

B.1.9   Remuneration committees should consider what compensation commitments (including pension contributions) their directors' contracts of service, if any, would entail in the event of early termination. They should, in particular, consider the advantages of providing explicitly in the initial contract for such compensation commitments except in the case of removal for misconduct.

B.1.10   Where the initial contract does not explicitly provide for compensation commitments, remuneration committees should, within legal constraints, tailor their approach in individual early termination cases to the wide variety of circumstances. The broad aim should be to avoid rewarding poor performance while dealing fairly with cases where departure is not due to poor performance and to take a robust line on reducing compensation to reflect departing directors' obligations to mitigate loss.

B.2 Procedure

Principle

Companies should establish a formal and transparent procedure for developing policy on executive remuneration and for fixing the remuneration packages of individual directors. No director should be involved in deciding his or her own remuneration.

Code provisions

B.2.1   To avoid potential conflicts of interest, boards of directors should set up remuneration committees of independent non-executive directors to make recommendations to the board, within agreed terms of reference, on the company's framework of executive remuneration and its cost; and to determine on their behalf specific remuneration packages for each of the executive directors, including pension rights and any compensation payments.

B.2.2   Remuneration committees should consist exclusively of non-executive directors who are independent of management and free from any business or other relationship which could materially interfere with the exercise of their independent judgement.

B.2.3   The members of the remuneration committee should be listed each year in the board's remuneration report to shareholders (B.3.1 below).

B.2.4   The board itself or, where required by the Articles of Association, the shareholders should determine the remuneration of the non-executive directors, including members of the remuneration committee, within the limits set in the Articles of Association. Where permitted by the Articles, the board may however delegate this responsibility to a small sub-committee, which might include the chief executive officer.

B.2.5   Remuneration committees should consult the chairman and/or chief executive officer about their proposals relating to the remuneration of other executive directors and have access to professional advice inside and outside the company.

B.2.6   The chairman of the board should ensure that the company maintains contact as required with its principal shareholders about remuneration in the same way as for other matters.

B.3   Disclosure

Principle

The company's annual report should contain a statement of remuneration policy and details of the remuneration of each director.

Code provisions

B.3.1   The board should report to the shareholders each year on remuneration. The report should form part of, or be annexed to, the company's annual report and accounts. It should be the main vehicle through which the company reports to shareholders on directors' remuneration.

B.3.2   The report should set out the company's policy on executive directors' remuneration. It should draw attention to factors specific to the company.

B.3.3   In preparing the remuneration report, the board should follow the provisions in Schedule B to this Code.

B.3.4   Shareholders should be invited specifically to approve all new long-term incentive schemes (as defined in the Listing Rules) save in the circumstances permitted by paragraph 13.13A of the Listing Rules.

B.3.5   The board's annual remuneration report to shareholders need not be a standard item of agenda for AGMs. But the board should consider each year whether the circumstances are such that the AGM should be invited to approve the policy set out in the report and should minute their conclusions.

C. Relations with shareholders

C.1 Dialogue with institutional shareholders

Principle

Companies should be ready, where practicable, to enter into a dialogue with institutional shareholders based on the mutual understanding of objectives.

C.2 Constructive use of the AGM

Principle

Boards should use the AGM to communicate with private investors and encourage their participation.

Code provisions

C.2.1   Companies should count all proxy votes and, except where a poll is called, should indicate the level of proxies lodged on each resolution, and the balance for and against the resolution, after it has been dealt with on a show of hands.

C.2.2   Companies should propose a separate resolution at the AGM on each substantially separate issue and should in particular propose a resolution at the AGM relating to the report and accounts.

C.2.3   The chairman of the board should arrange for the chairmen of the audit, remuneration and nomination committees to be available to answer questions at the AGM.

C.2.4   Companies should arrange for the Notice of the AGM and related papers to be sent to shareholders at least 20 working days before the meeting.

D.   Accountability and audit

D.1   Financial reporting

Principle

The board should present a balanced and understandable assessment of the company's position and prospects.

Code provisions

D.1.1   The directors should explain their responsibility for preparing the accounts and there should be a statement by the auditors about their reporting responsibilities.

D.1.2   The board's responsibility to present a balanced and understandable assessment extends to interim and other price-sensitive public reports and reports to regulators as well as to information required to be presented by statutory requirements.

D.1.3   The directors should report that the business is a going concern, with supporting assumptions or qualifications as necessary.

D.2 Internal Control

Principle

The board should maintain a sound system of internal control to safeguard shareholders' investment and the company's assets.

Code provisions

D.2.1   The directors should, at least annually, conduct a review of the effectiveness of the group's system of internal controls and should report to shareholders that they have done so. The review should cover all controls, including financial, operational and compliance controls and risk management.

D.2.2   Companies which do not have an internal audit function should from time to time review the need for one.

D.3 Audit committee and auditors

Principle

The board should establish formal and transparent arrangements for considering how they should apply the financial reporting and internal control principles and for maintaining an appropriate relationship with the company's auditors.

Code provisions

D.3.1   The board should establish an audit committee of at least three directors, all non-executive, with written terms of reference which deal clearly with its authority and duties. The members of the committee, a majority of whom should be independent non-executive directors, should be named in the report and accounts.

D.3.2   The duties of the audit committee should include keeping under review the scope and results of the audit and its cost effectiveness and the independence and objectivity of the auditors. Where the auditors also supply a substantial volume of non-audit services to the company, the committee should keep the nature and extent of such services under review, seeking to balance the maintenance of objectivity and value for money.

Part 2 Code of best practice

Section 2 – Institutional shareholders

E. Institutional investors

E.1 Shareholder voting

Principle

Institutional shareholders have a responsibility to make considered use of their votes.

Code provisions

E.1.1   Institutional shareholders should endeavour to eliminate unnecessary variations in the criteria which each applies to the corporate governance arrangements and performance of the companies in which they invest.

E.1.2   Institutional shareholders should, on request, make available to their clients information on the proportion of resolutions on which votes were cast and non-discretionary proxies lodged.

E.1.3   Institutional shareholders should take steps to ensure that their voting intentions are being translated into practice.

E.2 Dialogue with Companies

Principle

Institutional shareholders should be ready, where practicable, to enter into a dialogue with companies based on the mutual understanding of objectives.

E.3 Evaluation of Governance Disclosures

Principle

When evaluating companies' governance arrangements, particularly those relating to board structure and composition, institutional investors should give due weight to all relevant factors drawn to their attention.

Schedule A: Provisions on the design of performance-related remuneration

1   Remuneration committees should consider whether the directors should be eligible for annual bonuses. If so, performance conditions should be relevant, stretching and designed to enhance the business. Upper limits should always be considered. There may be a case for part payment in shares to be held for a significant period.

2   Remuneration committees should consider whether the directors should be eligible for benefits under long-term incentive schemes. Traditional share option schemes should be weighed against other kinds of long-term incentive scheme. In normal circumstances, shares granted or other forms of deferred remuneration should not vest, and options should not be exercisable, in under three years. Directors should be encouraged to hold their shares for a further period after vesting or exercise, subject to the need to finance any costs of acquisition and associated tax liability.

3   Any new long-term incentive schemes which are proposed should be approved by shareholders and should preferably replace existing schemes or at least form part of a well considered overall plan, incorporating existing schemes. The total rewards potentially available should not be excessive.

4   Payouts or grants under all incentive schemes, including new grants under existing share option schemes, should be subject to challenging performance criteria reflecting the company's objectives. Consideration should be given to criteria which reflect the company's performance relative to a group of comparator companies in some key variables such as total shareholder return.

5.   Grants under executive share option and other long-term incentive schemes should normally be phased rather than awarded in one large block.

6.   Remuneration committees should consider the pension consequences and associated costs to the company of basic salary increases and other changes in remuneration, especially for directors close to retirement.

7.   In general, neither annual bonuses nor benefits in kind should be pensionable.

Schedule B: Provisions on what should be included in the remuneration report

1. The report should include full details of all elements in the remuneration package of each individual director by name, such as basic salary, benefits in kind, annual bonuses and long-term incentive schemes including share options.

2. Information on share options, including SAYE options, should be given for each director in accordance with the recommendations of the Accounting Standards Board's Urgent Issues Task Force Abstract 10 and its successors.

3. If grants under executive share option or other long-term incentive schemes are awarded in one large block rather than phased. the report should explain and justify.

4. Also included in the report should be pension entitlements earned by each individual director during the year, disclosed on one of the alternative bases recommended by the Faculty of Actuaries and the Institute of Actuaries and included in the Stock Exchange Listing Rules. Companies may wish to make clear that the transfer value represents a liability of the company, not a sum paid or due to the individual.

5 If annual bonuses or benefits in kind are pensionable the report should explain and justify.

6. The amounts received by, and commitments made to, each director under 1, 2 and 4 above should be subject to audit.

7. Any service contracts which provide for, or imply, notice periods in excess of one year (or any provisions for pre determined compensation on termination which exceed one year's salary and benefits) should be disclosed and the reasons for the longer notice periods explained.

Book list

Taxation of directors and employees (Accountancy Books), 1995
Croner Publications, *Reference Book for the Self-Employed and Smaller Businesses (loose-leaf),* Updated annually
Institute of Directors
Directors Manual (looseleaf)
Corporate Governance series
The Remuneration of Executive Directors
The Board and the Auditors
Share Ownership for Employees and Directors
The Board and Consumer Protection
Directors' Personal Liabilities
Environmental Protection Law
Nominee Directors
Directors and Financial Management
Trading Through Subsidiaries
The Director's Appointment
The Non-Executive Director
Director's Guide series
Director's Guide to the Commercial Property Rates
Director's Guide to Employee Benefits
Director's Guide to Financing Growth
Director's Guide to Company Insurance
Director's Guide to Accounting and Auditing
The PricewaterhouseCoopers *Manual of Accounting,* Gee (Looseleaf, updated three times a year)
Kelly, B, Company Law for us and how to..., ICSA Publishing (1990)
Loose, P, and Yelland, J, *The Company Director/*Jordan, 1993
Lai, Jerry P.L, Martin, Steven; Ganide, Claire, *Company Secretary's handbook,* Tolley, 1996
Clayton, Patricia, *Forming a limited company,* Kogan Page (1997)
Butterworths rights and duties of directors, Butterworth Law (1996)
Doyle, L, *Directors Personal Liability,* FT Law and Tax (1997)
Roberts, D, *How to Form a Company,* 3rd Edition, ICSA Publishing (1991)
Ryan, C.L, *Directors: Liabilities, Rights and Duties,* 3rd Edition, CCH Editions, (1990).
Sealy, L.J. *Disqualification and Personal Liability of Directors,* 3rd Edition, CCH Editions, 1993
ICSA, *Company Secretarial Practice: Manual of ICSA,* ICSA/Woodhead-Faulkner.
Hyatt, Michael, *Single Shareholder company manual,* FT Law and Tax (1995)

Index

Accounting records
  best practice 95–6
  computers 97
  contents 95
  criminal liabilities 99
  data protection 97
  directors' duties 59, 94–9, 195
  disqualification 180
  financial services 97
  inspection 98–9
  legal requirements 94–7, 99
  located abroad 98
  retention 97–8
  see also Financial statements
Accounting Standards Board 91, 149
Administrative receivers *see*
  Receivers
Administrators
  appointment 201, 202, 203–4
  duties 204
Alternate directors
  appointment 44–5, 60
  Table A 44, 45
Alternative Investment Market (AIM)
  directors' interests 73–4
  directors' remuneration 132
Annual general meetings *see under*
  Meetings
Appointment
  administrators 201, 202, 203–4
  auditors 25–9, 31
  company secretaries 23, 25
  directors *see* Directors'
    appointment
  inspectors 187
  liquidators 208, 210–1
  office holders 195
  official receivers 210
  receivers 201, 202, 205–6
Articles of association
  Combined Code 14

  contents 12–14
  directors' duties 13–14, 57
  dividends 104
  Table A *see* Table A
  weighted voting 165
Assets
  directors' duties 65, 74
  non-cash 71–2, 146
  ownership 21
Auditing Practices Board 30
Auditors
  appointment 25–9, 31
  change 28–9
  Combined Code 259
  disclosure 29, 30
  disqualification 28
  dormant companies 26
  duties 30–1
  elective resolutions 26, 120
  eligibility 27–8
  engagement letter 27, 31
  financial difficulties, advice 195–6
  information requirements 31, 88,
    98–9
  officers 22
  ordinary resolutions 27
  registration 28
  removal 28–9, 115
  reports 29, 30, 31, 99, 149
  small companies 26–7
  statements on cessation 29
Audits
  benefits 31–2
  committees 86, 101, 102, 273–4
  exemptions 93, 100
  financial statements 92, 100
  internal 101–2
  meaning 29
  standards 29, 30

Board meetings
  absence abroad 80, 81
  agenda 82
  attendance 67, 84
  background papers 82, 266
  chairman 82–3, 87, 264–5
  Combined Code 57, 79, 85, 263–7
  committees
    audit 86, 101, 102, 262, 273–4
    nominations 48, 85–6, 266
    remuneration 49, 86, 125, 126,
      268–70
    routine business 83, 85
  duty of care 66, 79
  exclusion 82, 84
  material interests 70–1, 80
  minutes 86–8
  notice 80, 81–2
  objections 87, 104, 149
  quorum 70, 79–80
  Table A 70, 79–87
  telecommunications 80–1, 85
  void 81
  voting 70, 83–4

Cadbury report 1, 2, 3, 4, 10, 14, 48,
      49, 53, 83, 92, 102, 125
Capital
  injection 202
  public companies 220
  return to shareholders 69
  serious loss 113–14
  statutory declarations 220
Cessation
  auditors 29
  death 168–9
  removal *see* Dismissal
  resignation *see* Resignation
  retirement 164
  see also Disqualification

Chairman
  board meetings 82–3, 87, 264–5
  casting vote 83
  Combined Code 264–5
  disagreement with minutes 87
  shareholders' meetings 83, 116
  signing minutes 87
Charities
  companies 17, 27
  donations 74–5
Cheques
  authorisation 59
  pay   229
Combined Code
  annual general meetings 262,
    271–2
  articles of association 14
  audit committees 102, 262, 273–4
  auditors 259
  board meetings 57, 79, 85, 263–7
  chairman 264–5
  company secretaries 25, 264
  compliance 4–5, 10
  directors' remuneration 125–7,
    261, 267–71, 276–8
  financial statements 92, 272–3
  full text 257–78
  internal control 61, 262, 266, 273
  nomination committees 266
  non-executive directors 48, 49, 265
  preamble 257–9
  principles 260–3
  re-elections 164, 267
  remuneration committees 268–70
  service contracts 53, 163, 268–9
  shareholders 262, 263, 271–2,
    274–5
Committees *see under* Board
  meetings
Common seal 18

Companies
advantages 215–16
assets *see* Assets
books *see* Statutory books
certificate of incorporation 9, 17,
218
charities 17, 27
common seal 18
criminal liabilities 22
databases 39, 41
disadvantages 216–17
dormant 26
formation 217–18
going concerns 41–2
information sources 38–42
investigations *see* Investigations
legal personality 9, 18, 21
limited *see* Limited companies
liquidation *see* Winding up
management 21–2
names *see* Names
off-the-shelf 11, 14, 17, 217
officers *see* Officers
private *see* Private companies
public *see* Public companies
small 26–7, 132
solicitors 23, 24, 32
striking off 212–13
types 218–21
unlimited 220–1
Companies House *see* Registrar of
companies
Company law
DTI consultation 5
legislation 19–21
scope 18–21
Company secretaries
absence 25
annual general meetings 113
appointment 23, 25
board minutes 86

Combined Code 25, 264
directors 24
duties 24–5
eligibility 23–4
Compensation
dismissal 166–8
financial statements 167–8
Computers
accounting records 97
data protection 97
millennium compliance 106–7
Conflict of interest
directors' duties 5, 43, 45–6, 68, 69
multiple directorships 43
nominee directors 45–6
subsidiary companies 69
Connected persons
definition 137–8
loans 137–8, 139
substantial property transactions 71
Contracts
business opportunities 74
contract for services 127, 130, 223
contract of employment 223,
226–7
duties 58, 61, 69–74
interests 69–74
liabilities 58, 71, 72
managing directors 61
objects clause 58
service *see* Service contracts
voidable 72
Corporate governance
Cadbury report 1, 2, 3, 4, 10, 14,
48, 49, 53, 83, 92, 102, 125
codes of practice *see* Combined
code
definition 2
Greenbury report 1, 2, 3, 4, 10, 14,
125, 126

Hampel report 2, 3, 4, 10, 14, 48,
   61, 83, 102, 125
Credit transactions 142–3, 255
Criminal liabilities
   accounting records 99
   annual general meetings 113
   board minutes, 86
   companies 22
   directors' interests 71
   disqualification 176, 183
   financial statements 103–4, 128–9,
      149
   foreign employees 237
   fraudulent trading 197–8
   health and safety 234–5
   indictable offences 76, 174
   insider dealing *see* Insider dealing
   legislation 20
   loans 144
   names 59, 213
   officers 22
   resolutions 122
   serious loss of capital 114
   shareholder directors 157
   statutory declarations 207
   summary offences 76, 174–5
   table of offences 245–51
   transactions 144, 149

Data protection, accounting records
   97
Datastream 41
Debentures, receivers 205–6
Deeds, Table A 18
Delegation, directors' duties 57, 58,
   85
Directors
   alternates 44–5, 60
   appointment *see* Directors'
      appointment

connected persons *see* Connected
   persons
de facto 43–4, 65, 173, 183
definition 43
disqualification *see*
   Disqualification
duration of appointment 52–3, 163
employees 43–4, 50, 128, 166–7
interests *see* Directors' interests
liabilities *see* Directors' liabilities
managing 47, 61, 62
meetings *see* Board meetings
multiple directorships 42–3, 49
names, letterhead 53
nominees 45–6, 129
non-executive *see* Non-executive
   directors
powers *see* Directors' duties
removal *see* Dismissal
remuneration *see* Directors'
   remuneration
resignation *see* Resignation
responsibilities *see* Directors'
   duties
service contracts *see* Service
   contracts
shadow 46, 173, 183
sole directors 126, 168–9
terminology 43–9
Directors' appointment
   age limits 37–8, 115, 163
   alternates 44–5, 60
   disqualification *see*
      Disqualification
   eligibility 37–8
   formalities 45, 49–50
   Forms
      10: 15, 49, 50, 218
      288: 33, 42, 45, 49, 50
   information requirements, 38–42
   managing directors 57, 61, 62

minimum number 24, 38, 168
multiple directorships 42–3, 49
nomination committees 48, 85–6,
    266
nominees 45–6
public companies 38
re-elections 164, 267
Directors' duties
    accounting records 59, 94–9, 195
    agency 65
    articles of association 13–14, 57
    assets 65, 74
    board meetings *see* Board meetings
    conflict of interest 5, 43, 45, 68, 69
    contracts 58, 61, 69–74
    delegation 57, 58, 85
    duty of care 65, 66–7, 79
    employees 60, 67, 223–40
    fiduciary duty 65, 67–8
    financial difficulties 195–6,
        199–200
    financial statements 30, 92–4,
        100–1
    general duties 65–9
    general meeting attendance 116
    insolvency 67–8
    interests of company 67
    internal controls 61, 94, 262, 266,
        273
    non-executive directors 47–9, 66–7
    service contracts 51
    shareholders 9–10
    standard of care 10, 66
    statutory duties 67
    strict duty 66, 68–9
    subsidiary companies 69
    Table A 57
Directors' interests
    Alternative Investment Market
        (AIM) 73–4
    business opportunities 74
    contracts 69–74
    disclosure 69–71, 83
    financial statements 71, 73, 74, 145
    general notice 71
    liabilities 58, 71, 72
    Listing Rules 72–3, 155, 158
    loans *see* Loans
    material interests 80, 130, 145,
        146, 147
    related parties 72–4
    shares *see* Shareholder directors
    transactions *see* Transactions
    voting 70, 83–4
Directors' liabilities
    cheques 59
    contracts 58, 71, 72
    criminal *see* Criminal liabilities
    de facto directors 43–4, 65, 183
    debts 196
    excessive dividends 106
    fraudulent trading 197–8
    indemnities 75
    insurance cover 75–6
    loans 144
    nominee directors 46
    non-executive directors 47
    personal guarantees 53–4
    secret profits 74
    shadow directors 46, 183
    sole directors 169
    striking off 212–13
    substantial property transactions 72
    ultra vires 11–12
    wrongful trading 198–200
Directors' remuneration,
    alternate directors 45
    Alternative Investment Market
        (AIM) 132
    Combined Code 125–7, 261,
        267–71, 276–8

committees 49, 86, 125, 126,
268–70
company disclosures 130–1
contract for services 127, 130
disclosure 1, 3, 45, 128–33, 261,
270–1, 278
emoluments 129–31
employed directors 128
excessive 180
financial statements 45, 128–9
guidance 125–7
Listing Rules 132–3
nominee directors 129
non-executive directors 127
pensions 128, 129–30, 131, 133,
150, 167–8, 277, 278
performance-related 261, 267, 268,
276–7
policies 268
professional fees 130
service contracts 128, 130
share options 156, 268, 276, 278
small companies 132
sole directors 126
Table A 127
Directory of Directors 39
Disabled persons, employment
224–5, 236–7
Disclosure
accounts *see* Financial statements
auditors 29, 30
controlling parties 150
financial reporting standards
149–52
interests 69–71, 83
Listing Rules 1, 3, 4, 132–3
loans 69, 138, 141–2
multiple directorships 42, 49
names 17
pensions 128, 130, 131, 133, 150,
167–8

related party transactions 149–51
remuneration 1, 3, 45, 128–33,
261, 270–1, 278
shareholder directors 112, 155–8
transactions 145–52
Discrimination, employment 224–5,
236–7
Dismissal
administration 205
Bushell v Faith clauses 165
compensation 166–8
employees 238–40
public companies 165
shareholders' rights 165
unfair 167, 239–40
wrongful 166
Disqualification
auditors 28
bankruptcy 176
companies' legislation 174
court orders 173, 180–1
criminal convictions 174–5
criminal liabilities 176, 183
fraudulent trading 174, 201
general misconduct 174–5, 181
investigations 190
legislation 19
meaning 182–3
minor obligations 176–7
misfeasance 177, 182
no disqualification ordered 179–80
relevant debts 183
shadow directors 173, 183
Table A 37
time limits 182
unfitness
conduct 179–81
court assessment 177–8
financial statements 177
insolvency 175, 178, 181–2, 205,
206

office holders' reports 181–2, 205, 206
wrongful trading 176, 182, 201
Dividends
articles of association 104
excessive 106
private companies 105–6
public companies 106
restrictions 105–6
DTI
accounting records 99
consultation on company law 5
financial statements 104
investigations *see* Investigations
Dun & Bradstreet 39
Duty of care 65, 66–7, 79

Elective resolutions *see under* Resolutions
Eligibility
auditors 27–8
company secretaries 23–4
directors 37–8
see also Disqualification
Employees
contract of employment 223, 226–7
directors 43–4, 50, 128, 166–7
directors' duties 60, 67, 223–40
discriminations 224–5, 236–7
dismissal 238–40
employment formalities 225–8
foreign employees 237
health and safety,
enforcement 234–5
record keeping 233–4
representatives 233
statutory duties 232–3
holidays 232
insurance cover 229–30
itemised pay statements 228

maternity rights 231
meaning 223
pay
deductions 229
holiday pay 232
methods 229
PAYE 228
statutory sick pay 230–1
pensions 229–30
recruitment 224–5
references 225
right to be employed 226, 237
self-employment 223
trade union membership 235–6
working time 235
Expenses
advances 140–1
Table A 127
Experian Ltd 39
Extraordinary general meetings 113–14

Fiduciary duty 65, 67–8
Financial difficulties
capital injection 202
directors' duties 195–6, 199–200
insolvency *see* Insolvency
options available 196–7
professional advice 195, 201–2
Financial services
accounting records 97
legislation 20
Financial statements
accounting reference date 34, 103
auditor's report 29–30, 31, 99, 149
Combined Code 92, 272–3
compensation 167–8
contents 100–1
criminal liabilities 103–4, 128–9, 149
defects 104

duties 30, 92–4, 100–1
elective resolutions 26, 94, 120
filing 101, 103–4, 132
format 100–1
fraud and error 30
interests 71, 73, 74, 145
legal requirements 91, 94, 100–1,
    103–4
loans 145
non-executive directors 49
remuneration 45, 128–9
responsibility statements 27, 92–3
shareholder directors 158
shareholders' rights 93–4
small companies 132
time limits 103
transactions 145, 146, 149–52
true and fair view 30, 91, 93, 101
unlimited companies 221
see also Accounting records
Financial Times Business Research
    Centre 39
Floating charges, receivership 202,
    205, 206
Forms *see under* Registrar of
    companies
Fraudulent trading
    criminal liabilities 197–8
    directors' liabilities 197–8
    disqualification 174, 201

General meetings *see* Meetings
Greenbury report 1, 2, 3, 4, 10, 14,
    125, 126
Guarantees
    directors' liabilities 53–4
    loans 138, 139, 142

Hampel report
    code of practice *see* Combined
    Code

corporate governance 2, 3, 4, 10,
    14, 48, 61, 83, 102, 125
Health and safety *see under*
    Employees
Hive downs, receivership 203

Indemnities, directors' liabilities 75
Information requirements
    auditors 31, 88, 98–9
    directors' appointment 38–42
    liquidators 211
    memorandum of association 10–11
Insider dealing
    insiders 159–60
    investigations 189
    legislation 20, 58
    meaning 158–9
    penalties 160
    price sensitive information 158–9
Insolvency
    administrators *see* Administrators
    directors' duties 67–8
    disqualification 175, 178, 181–2,
        205, 206
    hive downs 203
    legislation 19–21
    licensed insolvency practitioners
        195, 201, 203, 206, 211
    liquidators *see* Liquidators
    office holders *see* Office holders
    receivers *see* Receivers
    reconstructions 203
    resignation 163–4
    trading
        fraudulent *see* Fraudulent trading
        wrongful *see* Wrongful trading
    voluntary arrangements 202, 204
    winding up *see* Winding up
    see also Financial difficulties
Institute of Directors 47, 125, 155

Insurance cover
  directors' liabilities 75–6
  employees 229–30
  employers' liabilities 228
Inter-Company-Comparisons 41
Investigations
  consequences 190–1
  court orders 188
  disqualification 190
  fraud 188
  insider dealing 189
  inspectors appointment 187
  instigation 187
  misfeasance 188
  ownership or control 188–9
  production of documents 189–90
  share dealing 189
  shareholders' rights 188
  types 187–9
  winding up 190

Key British Enterprises 40
Kompass 40

Legal personality, companies 9
Liabilities
  criminal *see* Criminal liabilities
  directors *see* Directors' liabilities
  insurance cover 75–6, 228
  limited companies 215
  relevant debts 183
  unlimited companies 220–1
Limited companies
  liability 215
  limited by guarantee 17, 219
  names 17, 59, 219, 220
  private *see* Private companies
  public *see* Public companies
Liquidators
  appointment 208, 210–11
  directors' misfeasance 201

  duties 208, 211–12
  information requirements 211
  provisional 210
  see also Winding up
Listing Rules
  directors' interests 72–3, 155, 158
  directors' remuneration 132–3
  disclosure 1, 3, 4, 132–3
  general obligations 18–19
  service contracts 112
  share dealing 155
  shareholder directors 155, 158
  transactions 73, 152
Loans
  assumption of liabilities 143–4
  connected persons 137–8, 139
  credit transactions 142–3, 255
  criminal liabilities 144
  decision tables 253–6
  definition 140
  directors' liabilities 144
  disclosure 69, 138, 141–2
  expense advance 140–1
  financial statements 145
  guarantees 138, 139, 142
  private companies 139, 141, 256
  public companies 139, 142
  quasi-loans 138, 139, 141–2, 254
  relevant companies 137, 139,
    253–6
  small 137, 139
  subsidiary companies 138
  third parties 138, 139
  see also Transactions
London Stock Exchange
  directors' appointment 49–50
  Official Yearbook 40
  rules *see* Listing Rules

Macmillan's Unquoted Companies
  40

Managing directors
  appointment 47, 61, 62
  Table A 61, 62
Meetings
  annual general meetings,
    attendance of directors 116
  Combined Code 262, 271–2
  criminal liabilities 113
  elective resolutions 111, 120
  frequency 111
  Listing Rules 112
  ordinary business 112
  purpose 111–12
  special business 112
  attendance of directors 116
  chairman 83, 116
  court orders 113
  directors *see* Board meetings
  expense advances approved 140
  extraordinary general meetings
    113–14
  location 115
  notice 114–15, 119, 120, 272
  personal representatives 117
  proxies 115, 117, 272
  quorum 115, 117
  requisition 113
  resolutions *see* Resolutions
  serious loss of capital 113–14
  shareholders' rights 111, 113
  special notice 114–15, 165
  Table A 111–17
  voting 118
Memorandum of association
  charitable donations 74–5
  information requirements 10–11
  objects clause 11–12
Millennium compliance 106–7
Minutes, board meetings 86–8
Misfeasance
  disqualification 177, 182

  investigations 188
  liquidation 201

Names
  business names 17
  change 17–18
  cheques 59
  criminal liabilities 59, 213
  directors, letterhead 53
  disclosure 17
  insolvent liquidation 213
  limited companies 17, 59, 219, 220
  public companies 220
  restrictions 16–17
Negligence, attendance at board
  meetings 67, 84
Nominee directors, appointment
  45–6
Non-executive directors
  Combined Code 48, 49, 265
  directors' duties 47–9, 66–7
  directors' liabilities 47
  directors' remuneration 127
  duty of care 66–7
  financial statements 49
  independence 47, 48–9, 50

Objects clause
  contracts 58
  memorandum of association 11–12
Offences *see* Criminal liabilities
Office holders
  administrators 201–4
  appointment 195
  liquidators 201, 208, 210–12
  receivers 201–3, 205–6, 210–11
  unfitness of directors 181–2, 205,
    206
  see also Insolvency
Officers
  auditors *see* Auditors

criminal liabilities 22
definition 22
secretary *see* Company secretaries
Official receivers
appointment 210
duties 211
Ordinary resolutions *see under*
Resolutions

Partnerships, disadvantages 216
Penalties *see* Criminal liabilities
Pensions
directors' remuneration 128,
129–30, 131, 133, 150,
167–8, 277, 278
employees 229–30
Personal guarantees, directors'
liabilities 53–4
Private companies
dividends 105–6
loans 139, 141, 256
sole directors 168–9
Profits *see* Dividends
Public companies
credit transactions 142–3, 255
directors' appointment 38
dismissal 165
distinguishing features 220
dividends 106
Listing Rules *see* Listing Rules
loans 139, 142
names 220
re-registration of private companies
34, 220
share capital 220
shareholders 169, 210, 219
sole directors 169

Quasi-loans 138, 139, 141–2, 254
Quorum
board meetings 70, 79–80

shareholders' meetings 115, 117

Ratification 68–9, 70
Receivers
appointment 201, 202, 205–6
debentures 205–6
floating charges 202, 205, 206
hive downs 203
official receivers 210–11
Registered office, location 15–16,
218
Registers
directors and secretaries 50
shareholder directors 112, 157–8
statutory *see* Statutory books
Registrar of companies
addresses 32–3
company formation 217–18
filing documents 24, 32, 33–4,
101, 103–4, 121–2, 132
forms
10: 15, 49, 50, 218
12: 218
43: 34
117: 34, 220
225: 34
287: 16
288: 33, 42, 45, 49, 50
363: 33
395: 33
652: 212
inspection of records 33, 39
multiple directorships 42, 49
removal of auditor 29
striking off 212–13
Remuneration
directors *see* Directors'
remuneration
employees *see* Employees
Resignation
circumstances 163

insolvency 163–4
procedure 164
Resolutions
criminal liabilities 122
elective
annual general meetings 111,
120
auditors, 26, 120
financial statements 26, 94, 120
notice 120
extraordinary 119
filing 121–2
majorities 118–19
ordinary
auditors 27
meaning 118
service contracts 52–3
removal of auditor 28, 29, 115
special
company name 17
ratification 68–9
when required 118–19
special notice 114–15, 165
winding up 208
written 120–1
see also Meetings
Retirement 164
Reuters Business Briefing 40

Service contracts
Combined Code 53, 163, 268–9
contents 50–1
duration 52–3, 163
duties 51
inspection 52, 53, 112, 129
Listing Rules 112
ordinary resolutions 52–3
remuneration 128, 130
retention 52
shareholders' rights 52–3, 112, 129
subsidiary companies 52

termination 53
terms of employment 50
wrongful dismissal 166
Shadow directors 46, 173, 183
Share dealing
call or put options 155
inside information *see* Insider
dealing
investigations 189
Listing Rules 155
notification 156
Share options 156, 268, 276, 278
Shareholder directors
call or put options 155
criminal liabilities 157
dealings *see* Share dealing
disclosure 112, 155–8
existing holdings 156
financial statements 158
Listing Rules 155, 158
notification 156–7
registers 112, 157–8
share options 156, 268, 276, 278
sole directors 126
subsidiary companies 156–7
weighted voting 165
see also Directors' interests
Shareholders
Combined Code 262, 263, 271–2,
274–5
company ownership 21
directors' duties 9–10
dividends *see* Dividends
institutional 262, 263, 271–2,
274–5
meetings *see* Meetings
public companies 169, 210, 219
ratification 68–9, 70
resolutions *see* Resolutions
return of capital 69
substantial holdings 14–15

Shareholders' rights
dismissal of directors 165
financial statements 93–4
investigations 188
meetings 111, 113
service contracts 52–3, 112, 129
transactions 71–2, 73, 146
unfair prejudice petitions 127, 191
written resolutions 120–1
Small companies
auditors 26–7
directors' remuneration 132
financial statements 132
Solicitors 23, 24, 32
Special resolutions *see under*
Resolutions
Standard of care, directors' duties 10,
66
Statements of Auditing Standard 30
Statutory books
inspection 59
meaning 14–15
minutes 86
registers 14–15
statutory requirements 241–2
Statutory declarations
share capital 220
winding up 207
Stock Exchange *see* London Stock
Exchange
Striking off 212–13
Subsidiary companies
conflict of interest 69
directors' duties 69
loans 138
service contracts 52
shareholder directors 156–7

Table A
contents 12–13
deeds 18

directors
alternate 44, 45
dismissal 165
disqualification 37
duties 57
expenses 127
managing 61, 62
number 168
remuneration 127
resignation 164
retirement 164
dividends 104
meetings
directors 70, 79–87
notice 114
shareholders 111–17
see also Articles of association
Transactions
arrangements 69, 71–2
credit 142–3, 255
criminal liabilities 144, 149
disclosure 145–52
financial statements 145, 146,
149–52
Listing Rules 73, 152
loans *see* Loans
material interest 145, 146, 147
no disclosure required 147–8
related parties 73, 149–52
shareholders' rights 71–2, 73, 146
small 73
substantial property 71–2, 143, 146
voidable 144

Ultra vires
directors' liabilities 11–12
ratification 68–9, 70
Unfair dismissal
directors 167
employees 239–40

Voluntary arrangements, insolvency
    202, 204
Voting
  board meetings 70, 83–4
  casting vote 83
  institutional shareholders 274–5
  shareholders' meetings 118
  weighted rights 165

Who Owns Whom 40
Winding up
  compulsory 209–12
  investigations 190
  liquidators *see* Liquidators
  petitions 210
  resolutions 208
  statutory declarations 207
  voluntary,
    creditors 208
    meaning 207
    members 207–9
Written resolutions 120–1
Wrongful trading
  contribution orders 198, 199, 200
  directors' liabilities 198–200
  disqualification 176, 182, 201
  professional advice 201–2
  statutory provisions 243–4

Year 2000 problems 106–7